Oxford
Hidden Walks

Victoria Bentata Azaz

To Yehu, dodi li, for walking beside me and holding my hand.
Thank you.

Published by Geographers'
A-Z Map Company Limited
An imprint of HarperCollins Publishers
Westerhill Road
Bishopbriggs
Glasgow
G64 2QT

HarperCollinsPublishers
1st Floor, Watermarque Building,
Ringsend Road, Dublin 4, Ireland

www.az.co.uk
a-z.maps@harpercollins.co.uk

1st edition 2022

A catalogue record for this book
is available from the British Library.

ISBN 978-0-00-849632-6

10 9 8 7 6 5 4 3 2 1

Printed in Great Britain by Bell and Bain Ltd, Glasgow

contents

introduction

Oxford is home to the oldest university in the English-speaking world and it is definitely a city best enjoyed on foot. Indeed, much of the historic centre is inaccessible to vehicles. It is also a very compact city, so nowhere is too far away. In fact, standing in the Cupola at the top of the Sheldonian Theatre in the heart of the University, you can see countryside in every direction.

This book aims to give you a flavour of the City of Oxford and its historic buildings, whilst leading you to green places you may not have realized existed; it is remarkable just how much green space there is inside the city. It also takes you beyond the city to enjoy some of the highlights of the county of Oxfordshire.

Many ancient villages are now part of the sprawl of modern-day Oxford. Amongst them we take you to Botley, Osney, Marston, Headington, Cowley, Iffley and Wolvercote. Beyond the city, you can explore nearby Wheatley, Garsington and Radley. Further afield lie Church Hanborough, Ducklington, Minster Lovell with its ruins and the pretty towns of Woodstock, home to Blenheim Palace, and Witney, once famous for its blankets. Further along the River Thames, discover Abingdon, which lays claim to the title of England's Oldest Town and was once the home of the MG car. Each place still preserves its unique character, its well-known landmarks and its secret gems.

about the author

Victoria Bentata Azaz is an Oxford City Green Badge tour guide and has been leading tours for over 10 years. She enjoys going for walks, meeting people, learning new things and discovering hidden places, particularly when these activities include tea and cake.

how to use this book

Each of the 20 walks in this guide is set out in a similar way. They are all introduced with a brief description, including notes on things you will encounter on your walk, and a photograph of a place of interest you might pass along the way.

On the first page of each walk there is a panel of information outlining the distance of the walk, a guide to the walking time, and a brief description of the path conditions or the terrain you will encounter. A suggested starting point along with the nearest postcode is shown, although postcodes can cover a large area therefore this is just a rough guide.

The major part of each section is taken up with route maps and detailed point-to-point directions for the walk. The route instructions are prefixed by a number in a circle, and the corresponding location is shown on the map.

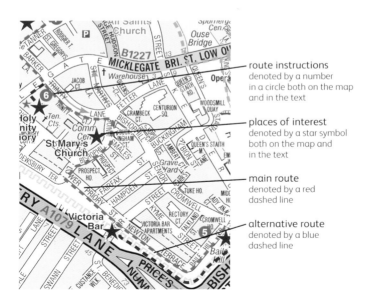

route instructions
denoted by a number in a circle both on the map and in the text

places of interest
denoted by a star symbol both on the map and in the text

main route
denoted by a red dashed line

alternative route
denoted by a blue dashed line

A̅Z̲ walk one

Secrets of the City Centre

Winding lanes and hidden gems in the heart
of the city.

This short walk starts right in the heart of Oxford at Carfax Tower and takes
in the historic centre whilst introducing you to some delightful winding
lanes and shortcuts that only the locals know. In the space of about an
hour, you can rub shoulders with a thousand years of history, starting near
the location of the ancient Littlegate and later passing the Saxon Tower of
St Michael at the Northgate and the remains of Oxford's Norman castle.
You will also see the University's imposing central ceremonial hall, the
Sheldonian Theatre, built by Sir Christopher Wren in the 17th century. You
will pass under the 20th-century Bridge of Sighs and Pembroke's 21st-
century glass-sided pedestrian bridge, and wind your way around the busy
city centre via some less-frequented lanes and alleys.

Refreshments are available in numerous pubs, cafés and restaurants along
the route of this walk, but the most secret is definitely the Turf Tavern, whose
entrance is to be found down a tiny alleyway, signposted 'An Education in
Intoxication'.

start / finish	Carfax Tower, Queen Street
nearest postcode	OX1 1ET
distance	2 miles / 3.2 km
time	1 hour
terrain	Pavements and paved paths.

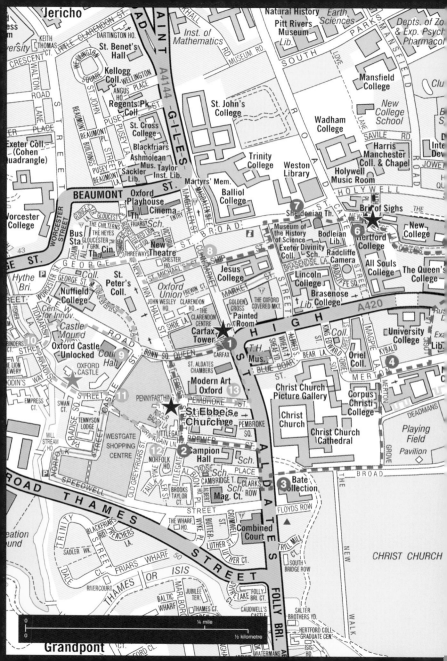

1 Start at Carfax Tower ★ and head along the left-hand side of Queen Street, away from the junction with High Street. Turn left down St Ebbe's Street and continue to the junction with Brewer Street, opposite the Little Gate plaque on the right hand-side of St Ebbe's where St Ebbe's becomes Littlegate Street.

2 Turn left down Brewer Street, go past Campion Hall and under the glass-sided Pembroke College Bridge. At the end of Brewer Street, turn right and continue down St Aldates to the pedestrian crossing beyond the entrance to Christ Church's Memorial Garden. Cross the road and turn left and then right through the Christ Church Memorial Garden gate into the garden, with Tom Tower and the Christ Church dining hall on your left.

3 Continue straight on, up past Christ Church's long Meadow Building and turn left at the end of the building. Go straight on until you meet a kissing gate. Go through this gate and along Merton Grove, emerging onto Merton Street through the gate at the end. Turn right.

4 Pass Merton College and turn left at Logic Lane, which goes right through University College. At the end of Logic Lane, opposite Queen's College, turn right into the High Street and cross over where it is safe to do so into Queen's Lane, to the right of Queen's College.

5 Pass St Edmund Hall and follow Queen's Lane round to the left between Queen's and New Colleges. It eventually turns into New College Lane.

6 If you wish, you could stop for refreshments by diverting just before the Bridge of Sighs down St Helen's Passage, a tiny alley to your right, and finding your way to the Turf Tavern. Otherwise, keep going and emerge under the Bridge of Sighs ★ onto Catte Street. Cross over to the square with the Sheldonian Theatre ahead of you and walk around it, exiting by a small arched gate in the wall onto Broad Street.

7 Turn left on Broad Street, pass the Museum of the History of Science and continue on the left-hand side of the road to Turl Street. Turn left down Turl Street, take the first turning on the right into Ship Street and walk to the end.

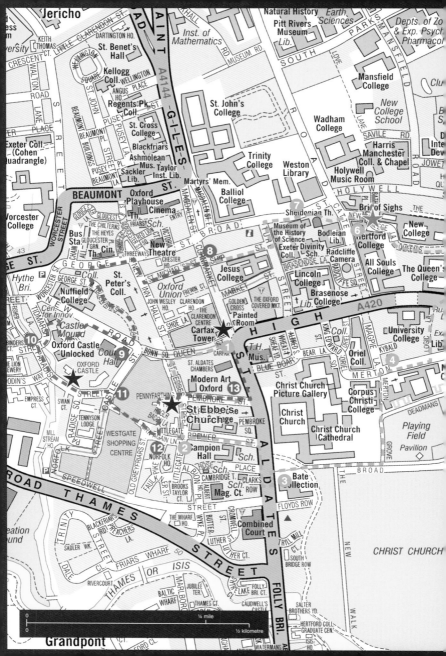

8 At the end of Ship Street, with the tower of St Michael at the Northgate on your right, cross Cornmarket Street into St Michael's Street and walk past the Oxford Union to the end of the road. At New Inn Hall Street, turn right and then left into George Street. Just after the Four Candles pub, turn left down the narrow Bullwarks Lane and left again where it goes upwards and becomes even narrower. You will come out onto New Road, with the Westgate Shopping Centre to your left.

9 Cross over at the pedestrian crossing and turn right down New Road. Pass the Malmaison Hotel entrance and walk to the entrance to Oxford Castle ★. Turn left immediately before the Castle Mound, walk through the courtyard and exit via a metal gate in the stone wall on the right past the Castleyard café. Turn left beyond the gate onto Tidmarsh Lane, which becomes St Thomas' Street, and cross Quaking Bridge.

10 Immediately after the bridge, turn left down Paradise Street. Pass Hare's Wharf and Paradise Square and the Jolly Farmers pub and at the end of the road, cross over Castle Street.

11 Turn left into the Westgate Shopping Centre, entering between the metal bollards to the right of the Social. Go straight across the shopping centre, exiting past the Roger Bacon plaque and the standing stones.

12 Cross into Turn Again Lane and take the first left up the narrow Roger Bacon Lane. At the end, turn right past St Ebbe's Church onto St Ebbe's Street and cross into Pembroke Street.

13 At the end of Pembroke Street, turn left onto the High Street, passing the Town Hall on your right and go straight on until you are once again at Carfax Tower.

₳Z walk two

Rivers, Meadows and Colleges

Green spaces and historical buildings in the city centre.

This walk starts right in the centre of Oxford at the intersection of the two main ancient routes through the city. What is most remarkable is just how quickly you can be surrounded by greenery. In less than 10 minutes, you reach Christ Church Meadow, a beautiful, peaceful spot featuring meadow, woodland and riverside walks. In summer you can see the college's herd of Longhorn cattle there and at all times of year, particularly early in the morning, you can watch the students setting off from the college boathouses to go rowing on the River Thames.

Glimpsing views into Oxford's beautiful Botanic Garden, you eventually come out onto Magdalen Bridge in the shadow of the college's magnificent tower. Continuing briefly down a suburban street you plunge into the Angel and Greyhound water meadow. Emerging in Bath Street, you head down the picturesque London Place, past the soaring architecture of the Oxford Centre for Islamic Studies and back again into a landscape of meadows, woods and water all the way to and through the University Parks.

On St Cross Street, you can survey the University's Science Area in one direction and head past some of the newest college accommodation in the other. Finally, you will return past some of the University's most iconic architecture. There are ample options for refreshments in the city centre.

start / finish	Carfax Tower, Queen Street
nearest postcode	OX1 1ET
distance	5 miles / 8 km
time	2 hours 30 minutes
terrain	A mixture of paved roads, parkland and riverside paths, which can get muddy after rain.

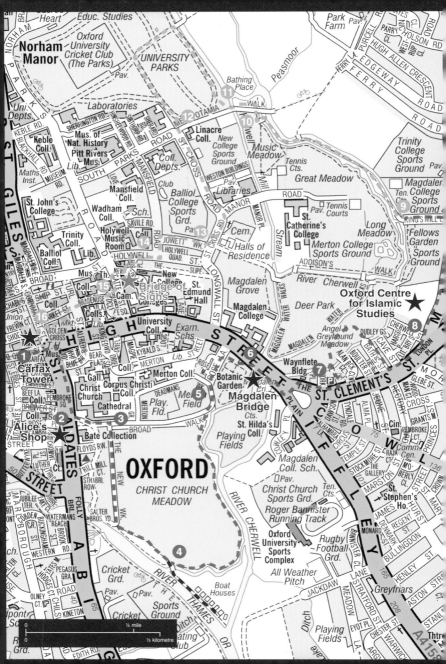

1 Start at Carfax Tower ★ in the very centre of Oxford. From the front of the tower, walk forward to the road junction, crossing over Queen Street and then St Aldates, and turning right to walk down its left-hand side, past the Town Hall and Christ Church's Tom Tower.

2 Turn left through the Christ Church War Memorial Garden gates almost opposite Alice's Shop ★ at 83 St Aldates. Continue through the garden and past the thatched shop further on to your right.

3 Beyond the shop, turn right to walk through Christ Church Meadow until you reach the River Thames. Turn left and head along the path in the direction of the college boat houses.

4 At the end of the path, you will see a bridge over the River Cherwell at the point where it flows into the Thames. For a diversion, you can continue over the bridge and look at the boat houses on the island, retracing your steps back over the bridge afterwards. From the bridge, continue on the path round to the left and follow it along the River Cherwell. Eventually you will pass between the Oxford Botanic Garden and Merton Field and come to a kissing gate at the end of Rose Lane.

5 Go through the kissing gate into Rose Lane and continue past the TS Eliot Lecture theatre on your left until you come to a drive to the right. Go through the gate beside the drive and walk along between the Penicillin Rose Garden on the left and the Daubeny Building on the right. When you come to the entrance to the Botanic Garden, turn left and exit through a gate onto the High Street opposite Magdalen Tower.

6 Turn right onto Magdalen Bridge ★ and cross the bridge. Just before The Plain roundabout, cross over and continue along the left-hand street, St Clement's Street. Pass York Place and turn left into a narrow alleyway between numbers 37 and 39 called Pensons Gardens. Walk under the bridge marked 'Alice House' to the end of the road and the gate at the entrance to the Angel and Greyhound Meadow.

7 Cross the small footbridge straight ahead and turn right into the meadow. Turn right through the gap in the foliage, cross the bridge and pass a children's playground on your right. Turn right across the field and cross another bridge into Bath Street. Continue along the street and at the end, turn left, back onto St Clement's Street and then London Place. Turn left onto Marston Road, past the entrance to Cherwell Street.

8 Continue along the Marston Road, passing the Oxford Centre for Islamic Studies (OXCIS) ★ to your left. Immediately after the OXCIS, turn left down a lane marked 'Private Road – Access to Kings Mill only'. Follow the road, with the wall of the OXCIS to your left and Magdalen College Sports Ground to your right.

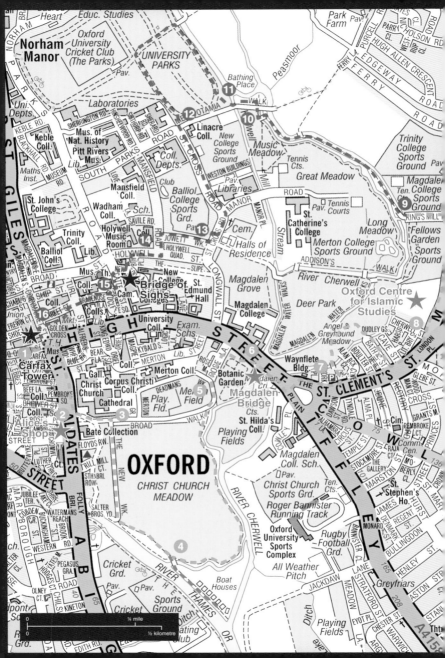

9 Go through the gate at the end and follow the path past Kings Mill and on between two bodies of water. You will pass over two bridges with weirs and finally you will reach a bridge on the left which you have to cross because the path ahead is a dead end with a locked gate.

10 After the bridge, turn immediately right and continue to the gate, cross the cycle path and go through another gate onto a footpath which goes left. Continue along this path until you meet another gate which takes you back onto the cycle path that you crossed after the bridge. Turn right and proceed to another bridge. Cross this and then go right through the kissing gate into the University Parks.

11 Continue straight along the path with the river on your right. At the steep footbridge over the river to your right, turn left. Continue along this path past a wooden-clad building on your right and tennis courts on your left. Just before the public toilets, turn left and continue until you reach the exit from the park. Exit onto St Cross Road beside Linacre College.

12 Turn left and continue straight ahead along St Cross Road. Cross Manor Road and continue round past Holywell Church. Cross the road at the crossing and keep going until you reach Jowett Walk.

13 Turn right down Jowett Walk. At the end, turn left down Mansfield Road. Pass the clocktower on your right and then turn right down Holywell Street.

14 Opposite Holywell Music Room, turn left down the cobbled alleyway, Bath Place. Go right up to the hotel and take the last gateway on the left through the Turf Tavern pub. Follow the path through the pub alongside the old city wall (or stop for refreshments!) and emerge via St Helen's Passage to see the Bridge of Sighs ★ to your right. Go under the Bridge of Sighs and then left onto Catte Street, past the Bodleian Library on your right.

15 Turn right into Radcliffe Square and continue round to Brasenose Lane. Head down Brasenose Lane until you reach Turl Street. Cross into Market Street and take the first entrance into the Covered Market. Inside the market, take the second turning right and continue across the market to the Golden Cross exit, which has a golden cross on a blue background on a shield above the exit.

16 Follow the path out of the market and along the Golden Cross arcade and exit onto Cornmarket Street. Turn left and you will shortly be back at Carfax Tower.

ⒶⓏ walk three

The Oxen Ford

Folly Bridge, Grandpont and the River Thames.

This short walk takes you along a little-known path from Abingdon Road, on the south side of the city centre, straight down to the River Thames at exactly the point where the University and its colleges have their boathouses. If you arrive at the right time, you can watch some college rowing whilst enjoying the view over to Christ Church Meadow. Crossing Folly Bridge, you continue along the Thames Path for a short distance before heading into Grandpont Nature Reserve and Park.

Grandpont, already a suburb in the 13th century, was so called because it was the location of a great stone causeway that allowed people to cross the Thames and its surrounding marshy meadowland. Where Folly Bridge stands today may even have been the location of the original 'oxen ford' which gave its name to the city of Oxford.

Attractive Grandpont Park skirts the railway line leading you to emerge across Dean's Ham Meadow, which is hidden behind the terraced houses of Marlborough Road. You will return to Hinksey Park, with its lakes and mature trees, where you can enjoy a picnic and a swim in the lido.

start / finish	Hinksey Park Car Park, Abingdon Road
nearest postcode	OX1 4PZ
distance	2 miles / 3.2 km
time	1 hour
terrain	This walk can get muddy, especially after rain.

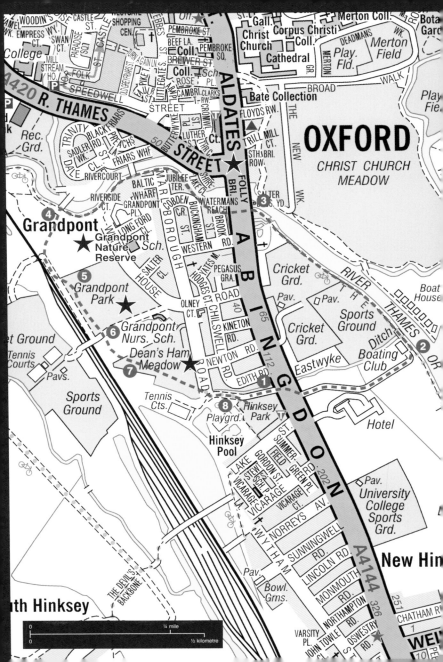

1 Exit Hinksey Park car park and cross Abingdon Road in front of the Hinksey playground. Take the first left almost opposite along the narrow path owned by University College. Follow the path down to the Thames.

2 Turn left along the towpath beside the University Boat House, opposite the college boathouses, and follow the river.

3 On reaching Folly Bridge ★, you have the option to stop for refreshments before crossing the road and continuing along the river path. Pass under the Grandpont footbridge and when you are nearly at the second bridge, the imposing iron Gasworks Pipe bridge, take the left fork and come up to the end of the bridge. Do not cross the bridge.

4 With your back to the bridge crossing, follow the path straight ahead away from the bridge, crossing a large area of parkland. This is Grandpont Nature Reserve ★. At the end of the path with the carved wooden fingers on the right, turn left at a T junction. Continue along the railway and at the next fork, take the right-hand path alongside some big trees with the railway behind you. Go down the steps and cross the wooden bridge. Go up the next set of steps. Come out and turn left into Grandpont Park recreation ground ★.

5 Go along to the right of the recreation ground to find another path. Exit at the right-hand corner onto a tarmac road with a car park on the right and a green railway bridge.

6 Turn left and follow the path along the railings and into the wood. The path turns left with a fence on the right. Continue straight on at the crossroads of the paths. At the next turning, take the right-hand path. Exit at the gate between a children's playground to the left and a fence on the right.

7 Cross a small wooden bridge and go between white posts into a large meadow, Dean's Ham Meadow ★. Follow the path round the right-hand side of the meadow, which then takes you left and through a gate to the end of Marlborough Road.

8 Cross the bridge on your right into Hinksey Park and turn left back into the car park.

ᴀZ walk four

The Devil's Backbone

Botley, Osney and Hinksey.

Starting at Oxford Railway Station, this walk goes through three apparently suburban areas of Oxford – Botley, Osney and Hinksey – but for most of its length barely passes a building. The Botley suffix *-ley* donates woodland, whilst *-ey* means island, and both feature, together with fields, parkland and a significant amount of water, in this delightful and surprising walk. What seems like an ordinary suburban landscape is suddenly transformed into open countryside and it is hard to believe that you are so close to the centre of a thriving city.

The colourfully named Devil's Backbone was so called because when the area flooded, little hillocks became small islands and their unusual straight line formation through the water made them look like vertebrae. It extended from South Hinksey to Oxford and was used by people in New Hinksey to get to St Laurence's Church in South Hinksey. Elongated today by the bridges over the railway and Hinksey lakes, it encompasses a variety of landscapes within one walk and also supplies some good views.

start / finish	Oxford Railway Station, Park End Street
nearest postcode	OX1 1HS
distance	4 miles / 6.4 km
time	1 hour 30 minutes
terrain	Mainly paths, which can get muddy. Some steps and one stile.

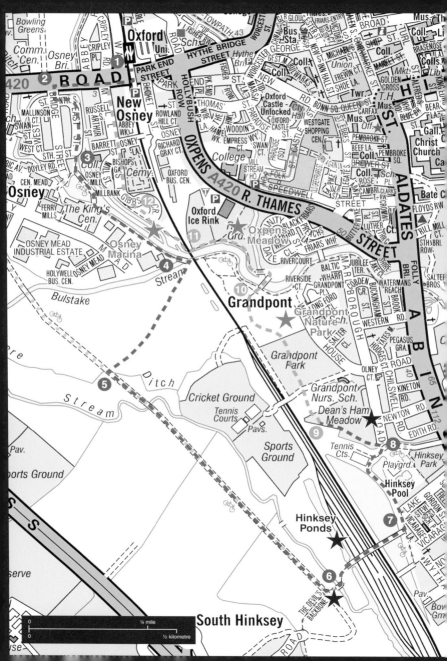

1 Turn right out of Oxford Railway Station onto Park End Street and walk under the railway bridge into Botley Road. Keep to the left-hand side of the road until you reach Bridge Street.

2 Turn left into Bridge Street and then left again down North Street, which curves round to become East Street.

3 Continue straight ahead on the path past the Osney Hydro-Electric Power Station to Osney Lock and over the bridge immediately after it. Continue straight on after the lock along the towpath for about 5 minutes to a bridge with wooden railings and a small obelisk memorial to Edgar George Wilson just before it.

4 Cross the bridge and turn immediately very sharp right onto a narrow wooded path. At the end of the path, cross over the stile into a field. Continue straight ahead diagonally across it and across the next field.

5 You will eventually reach an old railway track, identifiable because of the concrete at its edges and because of its straight line. Turn left along the track and keep going straight on for about three-quarters of a mile.

6 When you get to a gate across the track, with some woodland beside it, turn left. This is the Devil's Backbone ★ . Cross a wooden footbridge and a bridge with metal rails. Pass Hinksey Ponds ★ and continue over Hinksey Railway Bridge, which is a high bridge with a good view of the railway. Continue over the bridge above Hinksey Lake.

7 After crossing the biggest lake, the bridge descends. Turn left through a kissing gate into Hinksey Park. Continue straight on, passing between the lake and the pond in the park. Go in an anti-clockwise direction around the pond, with the tennis court to your left and alongside huge pine trees.

8 Turn left through the gate out of Hinksey Park and cross the bridge into Marlborough Road. Turn immediately left and walk diagonally across Dean's Ham Meadow ★ . Go between the white posts and into the wood across a small wooden bridge.

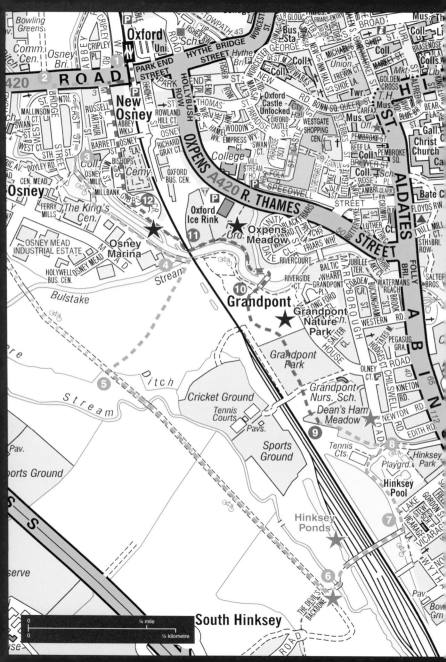

9 Go straight on where the paths cross and continue through the wood. Cross a metalled road and go straight across the recreation ground and down the path by the dog waste bin. Cross the concrete bridge and go to the left. Take the right fork at the end and cross Grandpont Nature Park ★ .

10 Go right to the Victorian Gasworks Bridge. Turn right across the bridge and then follow the spiral path down to the Green Bridge signposted to 'Botley Road'. Continue to Oxpens Meadow ★ beside the Ice Rink and keep to the left of the metal railings.

11 Go under two railway bridges and alongside the railway on your right and Osney Marina ★ on your left. Turn left past some red brick buildings on your right and cross a green to Gibbs Crescent.

12 Cross Gibbs Crescent, exit it and pass the entrance to Osney Marina with a large cemetery on your right. Continue along Mill Street to Botley Road, and turn right to return to the station. There are places to stop for refreshments in this area.

AZ walk five

Architectural Wonders

The Radcliffe Observatory Quarter and Jericho.

From Victorian working-class terraced houses in suburban Jericho to striking modern buildings near the city centre, this walk illustrates the fascinating variety of Oxford's architecture. The first remarkable sight is the Blavatnik School of Government, which rises like a huge glass wedding cake opposite the Corinthian columns of the Oxford University Press. Beyond it the 18th-century octagonal tower of the Radcliffe Observatory rubs shoulders with the ultra-modern Mathematical Institute. On Woodstock Road, incongruously squeezed in beside a traditional Victorian house, is Zaha Hadid's extraordinary, silver Investcorp Building, looking rather like an alien spaceship which has lost its way. Heading through Park Town, a genteel development in decaying Bath Stone, you eventually reach Lady Margaret Hall, with its grand new entrance.

The University Parks provide a calming dose of greenery before you marvel at the Physics Department's state-of-the-art Beecroft Building, the 'Victorian Zebra' of Keble College and the gothic splendour of the Natural History Museum. Mansfield Road provides a similarly delightful clash of architectural cultures, before you reach the iconic reaches of Broad Street and enjoy a further exploration of Jericho.

start / finish	Walton Well Road Car Park (Port Meadow South)
nearest postcode	OX2 6ED
distance	4 miles / 6.4 km
time	2 hours
terrain	Pavements and good paths.

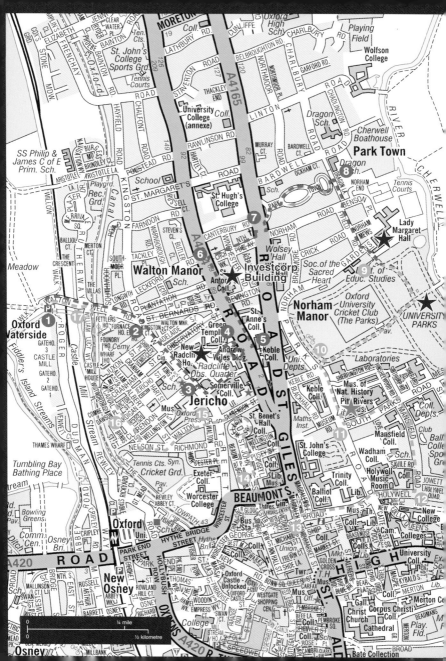

1 Turn right out of the Walton Well Road car park at Port Meadow South and go over the railway bridge into Walton Well Road. Keep going straight on until you get to Walton Street.

2 Turn right into Walton Street and continue until you get to the round Blavatnik School of Government Building opposite the Corinthian-columned main entrance to Oxford University Press.

3 Turn left down the walkway immediately after the Blavatnik, into the Radcliffe Observatory Quarter ★ . Walk with the red-brick Somerville College to your right until you are opposite the octagonal tower of the Radcliffe Observatory. Turn left and walk towards it. At the Observatory, with the statue of Dr John Radcliffe in front of it, turn right past the Alchemical Tree and the Andrew Wiles Building of the Mathematical Institute.

4 At the end of the drive, just before the exit onto Woodstock Road, turn right with the stone wall to your left and then immediately right again. You will now have St Luke's Chapel on your left. Continue to the front of the Mathematics Institute to see the Penrose Paving, then turn left to pass in front of the old Radcliffe Infirmary Buildings and exit the courtyard left past the statue of Triton in the water feature.

5 Turn left onto Woodstock Road, cross over at the pedestrian crossing and walk left up the right-hand side of the road, passing St Anne's College and noticing the extraordinary silver Zaha Hadid Investcorp Building ★ on your right further on.

6 At the pedestrian crossing, just before St Margaret's Church, turn right down a narrow alley called Church Walk and go straight on. Cross Winchester Road into North Parade Avenue and continue to the end. Turn left onto Banbury Road and cross over at the pedestrian crossing and continue left.

7 Turn right into Park Town and continue round to the right, taking either fork where the road bifurcates to end up at a small wooded area at the end and go straight on along the central path, then straight on under a stone arch marked 'The Terrace'.

8 Exit Park Town onto Dragon Lane at the far end and turn right. Continue down Dragon Lane and at the white gate at the end, turn right into Norham Road and then almost immediately left into Fyfield Road. Continue straight on, crossing the end of Norham Gardens and passing the front entrance to Lady Margaret Hall ★ . Ahead is a brick-lined alley, continue straight ahead down the alley into the University Parks ★ .

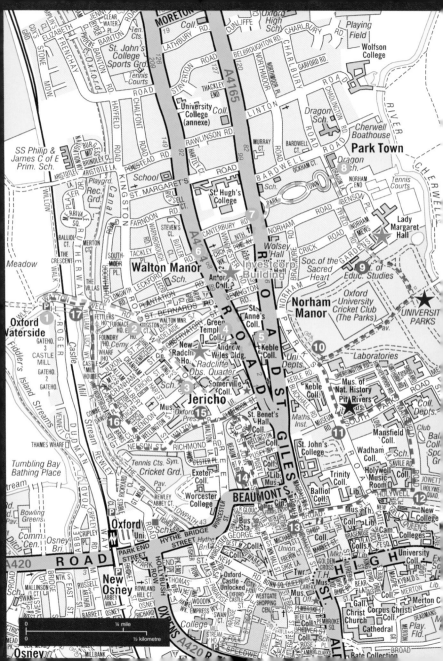

9 Take the right fork in the path ahead and go straight on, continuing straight on where the paths cross to the centre of the Parks along the path, then turn next right and walk past the Cricket Pavilion.

10 Exit the University Parks at Parks Road and turn left past the Beecroft Building of the Physics Department. Pass the Natural History Museum to your left ★ .

11 At South Parks Road, turn left past the Chemistry Buildings to the left (with the turquoise-domed Rhodes House across the road on the right). Cross at the pedestrian crossing past the Dyson Perrins Laboratory, retrace your steps and turn down Mansfield Road, passing the University Club and Harris Manchester College with its clocktower.

12 At the end of Mansfield Road, turn right down Holywell Street, passing the Holywell Music Room to your right.At the crossroads, cross Parks Road into Broad Street. Continue along Broad Street, passing the Sheldonian Theatre on the left, Blackwells bookshop, Trinity College and Balliol College to your right.

13 At the end of Broad Street, cross Magdalen Street and turn right. Opposite St Mary Magdalen Church, look for the entrance to a small alley on the left called Friars Entry and continue down it. At the end, turn right into Gloucester Street and at Beaumont Street, cross over and go almost immediately left into St John's Street.

14 Continue up St John's Street to Wellington Square and go to the right until you get to the University Offices. Exit Wellington Square past the University Offices and turn left onto Little Clarendon Street.

15 At the end of the street, cross Walton Street into Walton Crescent and continue straight ahead to the junction with Richmond Road. Pass the Synagogue on your left and continue down Nelson Street. At the end, turn right into Canal Street and continue past St Barnabas Church and tower.

16 Continue straight ahead down Canal Street past the Old Bookbinders pub and at the very end, where there is a small, paved park, take the steps sharp left up to the bridge. Cross the bridge over the canal and turn right along the Oxford Canal towpath.

17 Continue until you reach a path to the left from the towpath. Go up the path and emerge at the end of William Lucy Way. Turn left over the railway bridge to return to the car park.

AZ walk six

A Walk along the Waterways

The Oxford Canal to Wolvercote and back along the River Thames.

Oxford stands on the River Thames and was built beside a crossing point for cattle. It has a large number of watercourses, including its canal, which opened in 1790 but was made largely redundant by the arrival of the railway in the 1840s. Starting in the city centre at the remains of the magnificent Norman castle, this circular walk takes you along the Oxford Canal, replete with decorated canal boats, all the way to the pretty village of Wolvercote. It then brings you back into Oxford along the River Thames, beside the beautiful and ancient Port Meadow, an area of land that has never been built on and which was mentioned in the Domesday Book.

You will pass the ruins of the 12th-century Godstow Abbey, the original burial place of King Henry II's famous mistress 'Fair Rosamund', which was destroyed during the English Civil War. There are opportunities for stopping off at any one of several charming inns along the way, and on a fine day, there should be plenty of people boating on Port Meadow and fishing along the side of the canal.

start / finish	Oxford Castle Mound, New Road
nearest postcode	OX1 1NF
distance	6½ miles / 10.5 km
time	2 hours 30 minutes
terrain	Mostly towpaths, which can get very muddy after rain.

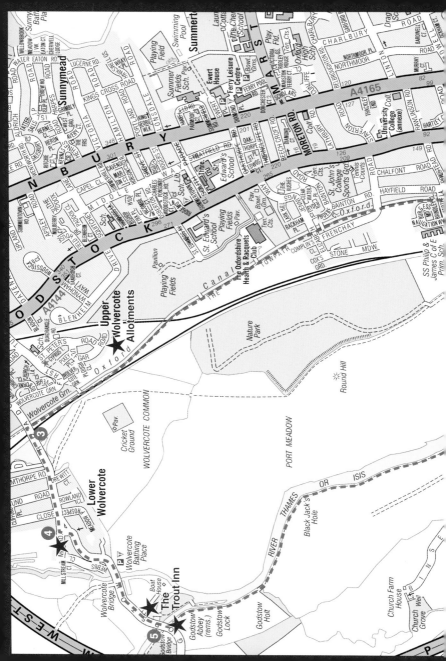

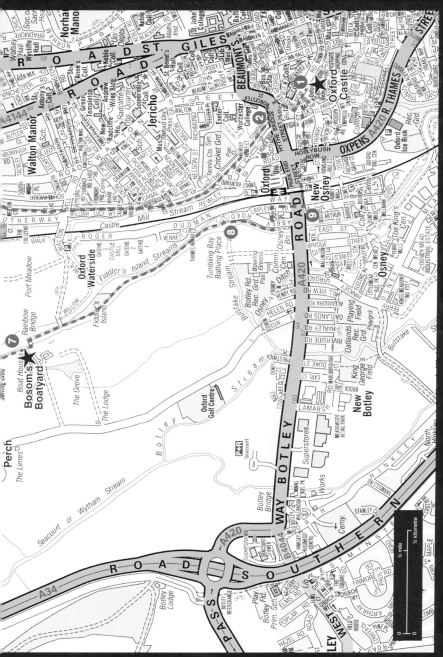

❶ Starting outside Oxford Castle ★ on New Road, with the Castle Mound behind you and Nuffield College facing you, turn left to walk along New Road until you meet a crossing at the bottom. Turn right into Worcester Street past Nuffield College and then cross at the next crossing to Hythe Bridge Street. Cross over Hythe Bridge Street, turn left and continue along the right-hand side of the street until you reach the entrance to the Oxford Canal towpath.

❷ Turn right down the canal towpath past the capstan (rope winder). Continue straight ahead alongside the canal for 3 miles (4.8 km), passing inhabited canal boats all the way along. Initially, you have the canal to your right and Castle Mill Stream to your left. Pass Worcester College's extensive gardens and lake, behind the hedge on your right across the canal. After passing over bridge no. 243 you see the Jericho Wharf regeneration project on your right and the striking campanile of the Basilica-style Church of St Barnabas, erected in the 19th century. As you continue through the suburb of Jericho, you pass the backs of its numerous Victorian townhouses. You eventually come to the playing fields of St Edward's School and then to open fields, beyond which are allotments on your right.

❸ When you reach the Grade II listed Godstow Road Bridge (you will see the number 235 inscribed above the arch), go under the bridge, past the lock gates and turn left back along a path up to the bridge. You will be on Godstow Road. Turn right over the bridge to cross the railway and go straight on. You will pass the Wolvercote Lakes on your right. Continue on into Wolvercote, where you can stop for refreshments at a choice of quaint pubs ★ either near the green or further on beside the canal.

❹ Turn left at the mini-roundabout just after the green to stay on Godstow Road. Follow the road past the Baptist Church on your left and continue over the Airmen's Bridge.

5 Pass The Trout Inn on your left and go across two bridges, then turn left through the gate signposted to the Thames Path. You will see the ruins of Godstow Abbey ★ ahead of you to the right. Carry straight on along the riverside path, passing the ruins on your right. Keep going through Godstow Lock and the field after it, crossing a small wooden footbridge at the end. Continue straight on with the River Thames on your left.

6 After nearly a mile (1.5 km) you will pass the path leading to The Perch ★ (a 17th-century tavern at Binsey). Continue along the riverside to a gate and go straight on past Bosom's Boatyard ★ on your right.

7 Shortly after the boatyard, cross the red footbridge to the left and continue past the wide bridge to Port Meadow on your left, taking the smaller wooden bridge ahead of you. The path now narrows and continues alongside the Thames. Keep walking for another 10 minutes along the Thames Path. You will pass a bridge on your left. Continue on to the benches in sight of the backs of some houses on the left.

8 At the fork after the benches, go right over a metal bridge and continue straight on. At a wide break between two houses, turn left. You will come out on Abbey Road. Cross immediately straight over into Cripley Place. Turn right at the end and walk down Cripley Road to where it ends at the main road.

9 Turn left onto Botley Road and go under the railway bridge, after which the road becomes Park End Street. Continue on to Frideswide Square, turning right at the roundabout in front of the hotel and then left to stay on Park End Street. Bear right at the end of the road into New Street. This brings you back to the castle, where you can spend some time exploring almost a thousand years of history in the Oxford Castle Quarter.

AZ walk seven

Quintessential Pursuits

Summertown, the River Cherwell and the University Parks.

Summertown is an affluent suburb in North Oxford and consequently has a wide variety of high-class eateries to enjoy either at the start or end of your walk. On Sunday mornings, there is also an excellent street food market to sample and enjoy.

Not far away is the River Cherwell, which you will follow for a time as it meanders its way gently southwards to the city centre. This shallow tributary of the River Thames is traditionally where people in Oxford go punting, and you will see the Cherwell Boat House, where punts can be hired, on the opposite side of the river just after Wolfson College.

This walk also takes in the University Parks, which are lovely at all times of year and provide a welcome break from the city. They are often the scene of much activity, however, with their cricket pitch and pavilion, tennis courts and opportunities for all sorts of other sports. In summer, they host outdoor plays and are a popular location for picnics and sunbathing.

start / finish	Summertown Car Park, Diamond Place (off Banbury Road)
nearest postcode	OX2 7BY
distance	3 miles / 4.8 km
time	1 hour 30 minutes
terrain	This walk can get muddy after rain.

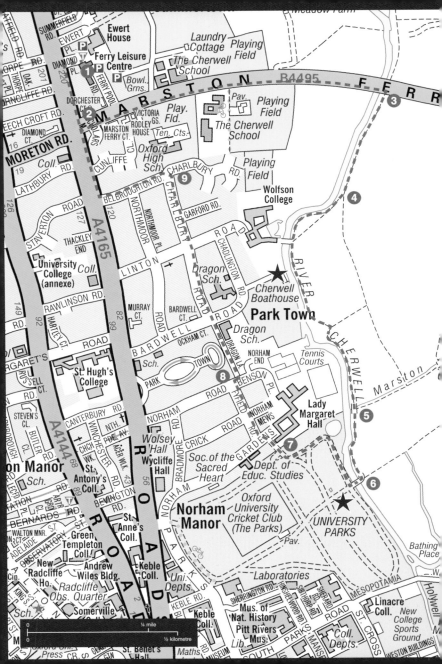

1 Turn left out of the Summertown car park or, if arriving by bus from the city centre, head south (back towards the city centre) down Banbury Road from Summertown Shops bus stop.

2 Turn left at the traffic lights down Marston Ferry Road, crossing to the right-hand side of the road. Pass Cherwell School and continue straight on for about 10 minutes, crossing a bridge with metal railings.

3 Immediately after the bridge, turn right down a footpath along the River Cherwell.

4 Continue straight on and when you reach a row of metal gates, take the right-hand gate (NOT the left-hand one marked 'Wolfson College Nature Reserve'). You will pass Wolfson College on the right across the river and the bridge that leads to it. Shortly afterwards you will also pass the Cherwell Boathouse restaurant and boat hire ★ on the other side of the river. Continue straight on, through a gate and across a small wooden bridge.

5 Where the path becomes impassable due to a stream, go left and then right across a boardwalk. Rejoin the path to the left, alongside the river. Pass the red-brick buildings of Lady Margaret Hall on the right across the river, which you will see through the trees. Cross a wooden bridge, a meadow, another wooden bridge and, opposite Lady Margaret Hall's punt

shed, a concrete bridge with metal railings. Continue through a metal gate at the end.

6 Go through a final metal gate, cross a bridge and turn right across the bridge over the River Cherwell, into the University Parks ★ . After the bridge, turn immediately right towards the pond. Just before the pond, turn left and continue, then turn left at the junction with another path.

7 Shortly afterwards, turn right out of the University Parks along a brick-walled alley, which will bring you out immediately opposite the Lady Margaret Hall (LMH) porter's lodge and in front of the main gate to the college. Continue forward along the right-hand side of Fyfield Road, passing a back entrance to LMH.

8 At the T junction, turn right into Norham Road and cross over to go down an alley next to house number 26, with a white gate at the end. This is Dragon Lane. At the end of Dragon Lane, cross Bardwell Road into Charlbury Road and go straight on, crossing Linton Road.

9 At the end of Charlbury Road, opposite Oxford High School, turn left into Belbroughton Road. Continue straight on and at the T junction turn right onto the Banbury Road. Continue straight on, crossing Cunliffe Close and Marston Ferry Road and return to the Summertown car park on the right or to your bus stop.

A͟Z walk eight
Headington Park Trail

Headington Hill Park, South Park and Bury Knowle Park.

Cuckoo lane, so narrow in parts that you have to walk in single file, is the secret way to bypass all the traffic and bustle of suburban Headington and its shops and head down to two of its beautiful parks.

Headington Hill Park, commissioned by a scion of the famous Morrell brewing family in the 19th century as the grounds to Headington Hill Hall, became a public park in 1953. Many trees from its original arboretum survive and details of the collection and a 'tree trail' are given on a board near the park's entrance.

Across the road, South Park is the regular venue for all sorts of celebrations including fairs and firework displays. From the top, there is a magnificent view of Oxford's dreaming spires. Exiting South Park, you enter part of Oxford's vast medical area, starting with the Warneford Psychiatric Hospital and, at the end of Hill Top Road, the Churchill Hospital, with its leading cancer centre, and pass alongside many medical research buildings.

Returning to the centre of Headington, don't miss Bill Heine's shark, incongruously protruding from the roof of a terraced house on New High Street. Finish the walk by enjoying Headington's Bury Knowle Park, a splendid location for Headington Library and the site of several wooden sculptures, before heading back down Old High Street, the original centre of the former Headington village, to the car park.

start / finish	Headington Car Park, Old High Street
nearest postcode	OX3 9HP
distance	4½ miles / 7.2 km
time	2 hours
terrain	A mixture of pavements and paths, which are mostly dry but can get muddy.

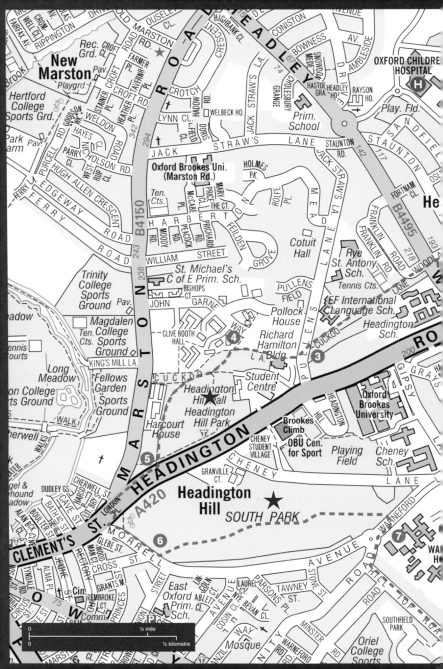

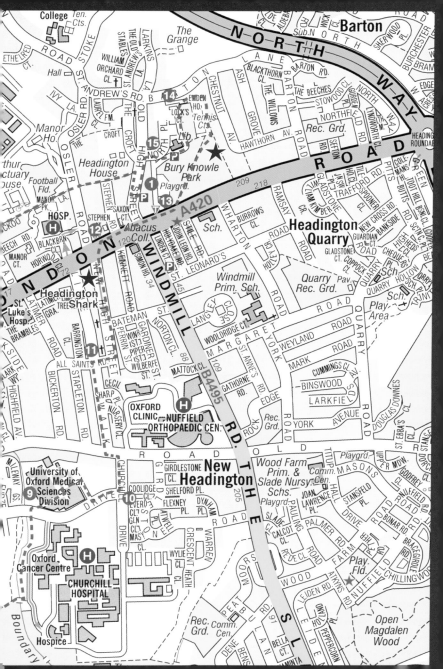

This walk starts at Headington car park on Old High Street, which may also be reached by bus, with several bus services from the city centre stopping at Headington Shops on London Road, near the top of Old High Street.

1 From the car park, cross over Old High Street and turn right. Look for the tiny entrance to Cuckoo Lane on the left, just before the tall trees. Turn sharp left to walk along Cuckoo Lane, passing under two low-arched bridges and crossing over Osler Road.

2 Cross Sandfield Road and go straight on. The road becomes Woodlands Road. Cross Headley Way into the continuation of Woodlands Road and go straight on along the left-hand path and between wooden posts to the continuation of Cuckoo Lane.

3 As you approach Pullens Lane, take the left-hand fork in the path. Cross Pullens Lane and go straight on, to the right of the wall. With the wall on your left, go straight on downhill and past the allotments on your right.

4 Where the wall ends and railings start, turn left into Headington Hill Park ★ . Follow the path straight on until you meet a tarmac path. Turn right and follow the path round the park until you get to the blue gates of the main entrance.

5 Exit the park through the blue gates and turn right onto Headington Road. Continue down Headington Hill and cross the Marston Road crossing, then cross over Headington Road towards South Park and continue to the right. Very soon, at Morrell Avenue, turn left and follow the park railings round until you find an entrance to the park with a fitness area to the left.

6 Enter South Park ★ and take the path in front of you which heads diagonally upwards across the park. At the clump of trees, go right and head for the bench. Keeping the bench on your right, head for the next two benches, the second of which is beside a lone tree surrounded by a wooden fence. Pass between the bench and the fenced area. Pass a fitness area and children's play area to your right and exit South Park at the gate in the railings onto Warneford Lane.

7 Cross Warneford Lane and turn right. At the roundabout, take the first left into Divinity Road, then first left again into Hill Top Road and continue to the end.

8 Turn left (signposted 'Footpath to Churchill Hospital'). Take the left fork across the meadow and at the end, take the right fork into a wooded area. Cross the bridge over the stream and turn left halfway along a house on stilts. Then take the left fork to continue along a woodland path for a short distance.

9 Arrive at Roosevelt Drive, cross over and turn left down a walkway past the Richard Doll Building. At the end of the walkway, turn left then immediately right past the green Old Road Campus Research Building, then turn right at the Kennedy Institute of Rheumatology and at the T Junction, turn left back into Roosevelt Drive.

10 At the next T Junction, turn left into Churchill Drive. Continue to the traffic lights at the end of the road and turn left onto Old Road. At the crossing immediately to your left, cross over, go left and shortly thereafter turn right into Lime Walk.

11 Continue straight on up Lime Walk until you reach All Saints Road. Turn right down All Saints Road and at the end of the road, turn left into New High Street, passing the church on your left. Notice Bill Heine's Headington Shark ★ on the left at number 2 as you head to the end of New High Street.

12 Turn right onto London Road and cross the road at the pedestrian crossing. At the crossroads, cross Old High Street and continue to the entrance of Bury Knowle Park ★ .

13 Follow the path diagonally across the park, continuing past the hedge at the top and past the tennis courts. Beyond the tennis courts, turn left behind the changing rooms just before the park exit to Chestnut Avenue. Staying in the park, continue straight on along the path until it turns left because of the stone wall ahead. Follow the path left and down a narrow alleyway with stone walls either side. It eventually goes to the left.

14 Go straight ahead through the Sensory Garden and exit at the far end. Continue forward and pass Bury Knowle House (Headington Library) on your right. Go through the car park and exit right and then turn left onto North Place.

15 At the end of North Place, turn left opposite The Croft back onto Old High Street. Return to the car park on the left or go straight on to Headington Shops.

ᴀᴢ walk nine

Historic Village

Old Marston.

Old Marston is a picturesque village now lying on the outskirts of Oxford, about 3 miles (5 km) northeast of the city centre. Its history goes back to the 12th century, when it was named for its proximity to the marshy land by the River Cherwell. It used to belong to the manor of nearby Headington. Arguably its most significant moment came during the English Civil War in 1646, when it was occupied by Parliamentarian troops under General Halifax. It was here in a house now named 'Cromwell's House' that the Parliamentarians and Royalists negotiated the Surrender of Oxford, which resulted in triumph for the Parliamentarians led by Oliver Cromwell. The walk passes the door, and you can see a blue plaque on the wall commemorating the event.

Two of Oxford's 'Penicillin scientists' lived in Old Marston in the 20th century: Lord Florey and Norman Heatley, whose blue plaque you can see by taking a detour to number 12 Oxford Road.

The walk takes you through the garden of The Victoria Arms, which has a charming view over the River Cherwell. As well as walking along the river, you will also follow Marston Brook and pass through some well-kept allotments. The route then takes you by two cemeteries of different vintages and past quaint old houses, some of which date back to the 17th and 18th centuries.

start / finish	Mill Lane, Old Marston (close to the entrance of The Victoria Arms)
nearest postcode	OX3 0QA
distance	2½ miles / 4 km
time	1 hour 30 minutes
terrain	This walk can get very muddy, so wear appropriate footwear. There are five stiles to cross.

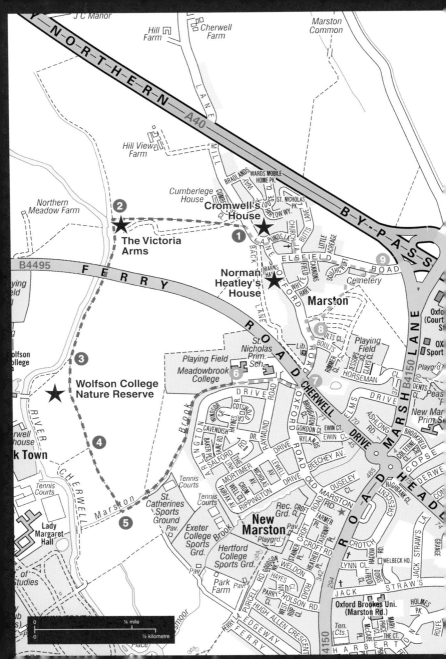

On-street parking is available on Mill Lane. Alternatively, the village is served by buses from the city centre.

1 The walk starts on Mill Lane, approximately 30 yards (27 metres) south of the entrance to the drive of The Victoria Arms pub (this is to your left as you face down the drive). Look for a public footpath sign and a gate. Go through the gate and follow the path. It will cross The Victoria Arms drive on the other side of the field through a gate. Cross The Victoria Arms drive and continue through another gate. Take the left-hand path along the side of the field. Continue through the double wooden fences at the end of the field and go straight on.

2 At the end of the field, turn left to find yourself in the garden of The Victoria Arms ★ . Continue across the back of the pub at the top of the lawn until you exit on a path to the right of the car park. Continue along this narrow shaded path for about 10 minutes and you will emerge at Marston Ferry Road. Cross Marston Ferry Road and continue straight on along the path beside the River Cherwell along the right-hand side of a large field.

3 At the gate to the Wolfson College Nature Reserve ★ , go through the wooden gate on the left, following the orange footpath sign. Continue along the left-hand side of the reserve, along a path which takes you right so that you exit the field from its centre. Continue along the left-hand side of the next field and exit far left along a narrow, hidden path.

4 Cross the stile into a wooded area and go straight on following the path. The path may become very muddy indeed. Keep straight on at a crossroads in the paths. Continue down the left-hand side of the field after the crossroads and exit via a kissing gate and across a plank to another metal gate. Take the right-hand path, which takes you down the left-hand side of four fields before you get to a concrete bridge over Marston Brook.

5 After the bridge, turn immediately left and follow the narrow path along the brook through a wooded area until you emerge to see a wooden bridge on the left. Cross the wooden bridge and turn right, continuing along the brook. Follow the path along the brook through a wooded area and alongside the backs of houses.

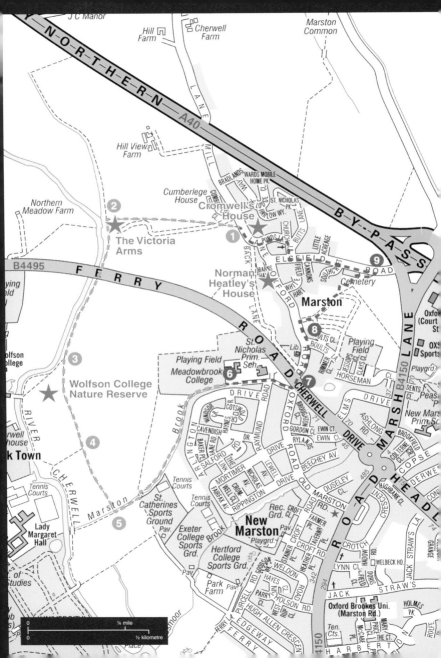

6 At the end, go through a kissing gate and straight on until the path ends by the entrance to Meadowbrook College. Continue straight on up the road ahead of you, past St Nicholas Primary School and follow the road to the right until you meet Cherwell Drive.

7 Cross at the pedestrian crossing over Cherwell Drive into Oxford Road. Continue down Oxford Road, passing Marston Library and when you get to the allotments on the right, turn right to follow the footpath through the allotments.

8 Inside the allotments, take the first left fork, then a right fork opposite some brown houses, then turn immediately left and spot the end of a very narrow footpath hidden in bushes at the end of the allotments on the right. Continue down this path, crossing a wooden bridge and a stile and follow the path left. The path will take you across a stile into the end of a private garden, where you need to turn right and exit by another wooden stile into a field. On the left, you will see the cemetery. You can either enter the cemetery, walk straight across it and exit by another gate (if the gates are open) or continue on the path along the back of the cemetery and then diagonally across and exit over a stile into Elsfield Road.

9 Turn left on Elsfield Road and go straight on until you reach Church Road. Turn right down Church Road past the cemetery and St Nicholas Church and then bear left into Ponds Lane. At the end of the lane, bear right into Mill Lane. Cromwell's House ★ is on the right. Continue round to the right to return to the start of the walk.

◮Ƶ walk ten

Village and City

From Iffley to Oxford High Street and back along the
Thames Path.

This walk starts and finishes in Iffley, a picturesque village within the city
boundary, with its ancient church, thatched cottages and the lock from
which the Oxford University rowing races start. It takes you across Florence
Park, opened in the 1930s to cater to East Oxford's burgeoning population
and today a haven of mature trees and well-kept flowerbeds, and Cowley
Marsh Park. From here you walk down Oxford's most multicultural and
arguably most interesting street, the Cowley Road, with its international vibe
and plethora of restaurants.

Continuing along Oxford's historic High Street, you encounter the University
in all its glory, passing England's oldest Botanic Garden, the Examination
Schools and several colleges – University, Queen's and All Souls – as well
as the University Church, the gathering place of the medieval university.
Continuing down St Aldate's, enjoy the iconic view of Christ Church's Tom
Tower before joining the River Thames and possibly watching some student
rowing. After following a glorious section of the Thames Path, the walk ends
back in Iffley, where you can spend time visiting its Romanesque church
before or after stopping off for some refreshment.

start / finish	Henley Avenue, at the junction with Iffley Turn
nearest postcode	OX4 4AS
distance	5¾ miles / 9.3 km
time	2 hours
terrain	This is a generally dry walk, but can get muddy if there has been any recent rain.

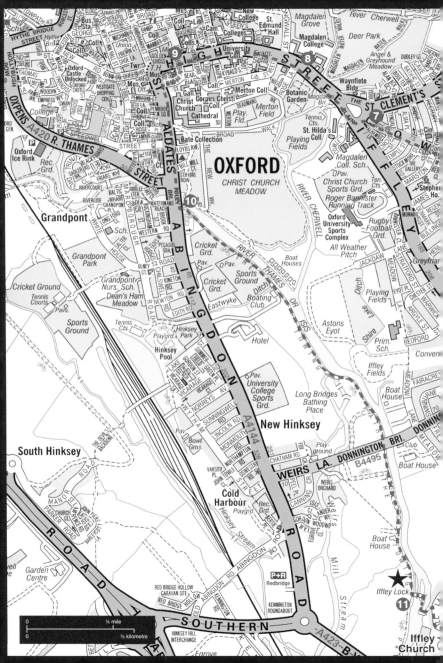

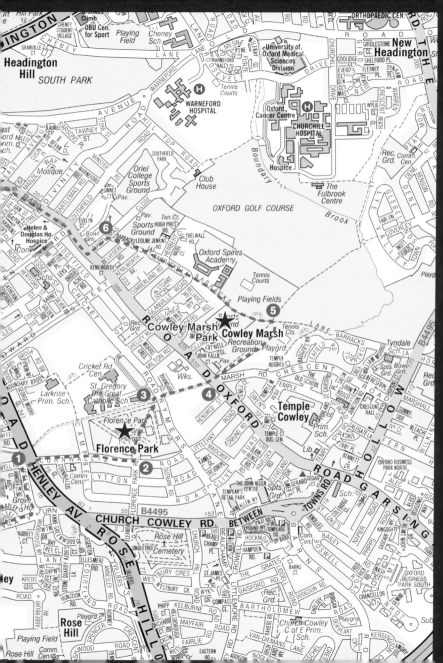

On-street parking is available along Iffley Turn, close to the start point. Alternatively, there is a regular bus service from the city centre that passes along Iffley Road and Henley Avenue.

1 Cross Henley Avenue (which is the continuation of Iffley Road) at the crossing close to the junction with Iffley Turn and go left and immediately right into Cornwallis Road. Walk on the left-hand side of Cornwallis Road past Campbell Road and turn left at the mini-roundabout, entering Florence Park ★.

2 Go straight ahead through the left-hand gate and take the second path straight ahead of the main gate. Go across a brick and stone bridge. After that, take the third fork in the path ahead and continue down an avenue of large horse chestnut trees. Walk past the Bowling Green on your right and after the bandstand on the left and the tennis courts on the right exit the park where Rymers Lane becomes Cricket Road.

3 Cross Rymers Lane/Cricket Road at the crossing immediately in front of you and go down the alley opposite. Continue straight on until you reach Cowley Road.

4 Cross Cowley Road where it becomes Oxford Road and go into Cowley Marsh Park ★ through the gate to the left. Continue up the path to the left of the corrugated metal building with the park to your left. Keep following the path as it bends to the left. At the basketball pitch turn left onto the intersecting path. Keep going left at the next intersection with a fence on the right and a children's playground to your left.

5 Exit Cowley Marsh Park onto Barracks Lane beside Oxford Spires Academy. Continue straight on along Barracks Lane, crossing Glanville Road and Cumberland Road. Eventually, the road becomes a path again. Keep straight on, following the sign 'City Centre Cowley Road'. Cross Kenilworth Avenue and continue between hedges on either side, passing a cricket pitch on the right.

6 On reaching Bartlemas Close, turn left and keep going until you reach Cowley Road. Turn right and walk along Cowley Road. You will pass SS Mary and John Church on the left and the Central Oxford Mosque in Manzil Way on your right beside the East Oxford Health Centre.

7 Continue past all the shops to The Plain roundabout. Take the third turning over Magdalen Bridge with the tower ahead of you.

8 Walk on the left-hand side of the High Street past the Botanic Garden, the Exam Schools, Queens College, University College, All Souls and the University Church of St Mary the Virgin. If you wish, there are places to stop for refreshments on the High Street or in the Covered Market.

9 Continue along the High Street and after the second pedestrian crossing, turn left down the very narrow lane called Wheatsheaf Yard. It is easily missed, so keep a look out for it.. At the end of Wheatsheaf Yard, turn right into Blue Boar Lane. At the end, just by the Town Hall on your right, turn left into St Aldates. Walk past Christ Church's Tom Tower. Continue to the bottom of St Aldates, past the Christ Church War Memorial Garden, the police station and the Head of the River pub to Folly Bridge.

10 Immediately after Folly Bridge, turn left down the tow path. Follow the Thames Path for 1½ miles (2.4 km) all the way to Iffley Lock. The Isis Farmhouse pub has a lovely view over the river.

11 Arrive at Iffley Lock ★ , cross the lock and the weir and continue along the fenced-in path beside the river, which goes round into Iffley. Turn left past Grist Cottage and continue until you reach Mill Lane. Turn right up Mill Lane and follow the road round to the left until you reach Iffley Church ★ . Either turn left – or, if you visit the church, then when you emerge, continue forwards – on Church Way past the Church Hall and the former Iffley Parochial School.

12 Go straight on through Iffley, passing the Community Shop and the Prince of Wales pub. Arrive at the mini-roundabout and turn left into Iffley Turn to conclude the walk.

A̶Z̶ walk eleven

Windmill and Hills

Wheatley Windmill, Shotover Country Park, Forest Hill and Wheatley.

This walk takes you past the handsome Wheatley Windmill, a notable landmark just outside the village of Wheatley, 6 miles (9.7 km) east of Oxford. The current mill dates back to the 18th century (though there were mills in this location earlier) and has an unusual and very distinctively shaped tower*.

There are good views from the lane leading from the mill and you gradually approach Shotover Hill, eventually taking the Old Road, which was a turnpike road in the 18th and 19th centuries. There is a great view over Oxford from the other side of Shotover's car park, so there is a brief stop to admire it before you turn back and head for Sandhills, one of the few places you can cross the A40 on foot via an underpass. You continue along the Oxford Greenbelt Way all the way to the village of Forest Hill, where you can admire more views before crossing back over the A40 to return to Wheatley.

*Note that Wheatley Windmill is a private property and is open only on occasional Sunday afternoons. If you wish your walk to coincide with an open day, check the website www.wheatleymill.co.uk

start / finish	Church Road Car Park, Church Road, Wheatley
nearest postcode	OX33 1LU
distance	6½ miles / 10.5 km
time	3 hours
terrain	There is a long, steady climb at the start of the walk. More than half of the walk is on paths, which can get muddy. There are three stiles to cross and some steps to climb.

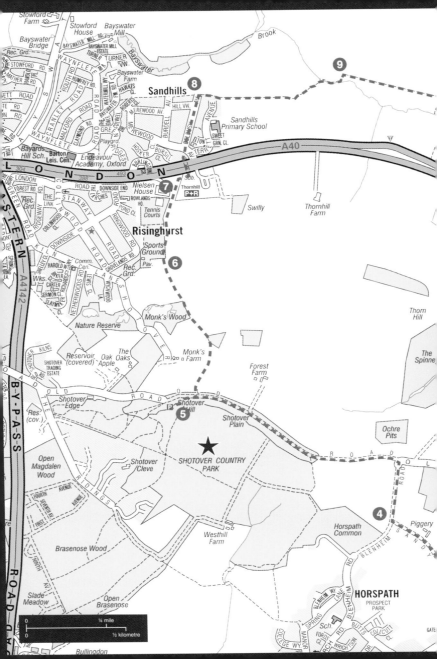

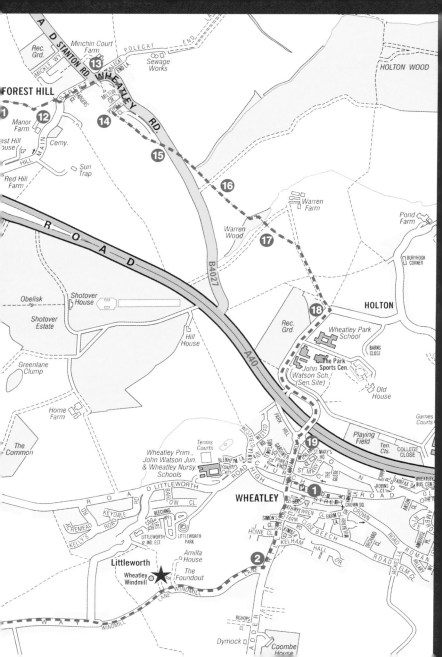

There is parking at Church Road car park, alternatively you could arrive by bus from Oxford city centre, which stops on Church Road.

1 Turn left out of the car park and then left again into Holloway Road. At the end, cross over High Street then continue on a steady climb up Station Road to your left, which becomes Ladder Hill. Proceed up the road and look out for a stone wall on the right ahead of you, with an embedded red post box. The lane just before this, on the right, is Windmill Lane.

2 Turn right into Windmill Lane and continue your climb as the lane narrows. Wheatley Windmill ★ is at the top on your right. You will also have some good views of Littleworth to the right further on.

3 Turn right along Sandy Lane marked 'Bridleway Shotover 1' between a house on the left and a field on the right. Pass a small gorge on the right. Continue past the Old Piggeries on the right.

4 At the T junction, turn right and at the next T junction turn left alongside a reservoir on the left. Go straight on and you will come to a sign proclaiming 'Shotover Country Park' ★ . Continue to the car park at the end and turn left for an open area of land with a bench and views over Oxford.

5 Retrace your steps through the car park and back up the track until opposite a clump of bushes, where there is a hidden entrance to a path through bushes to your left. Go through the kissing gate to a narrow path and straight on with a field on your right and a wood on your left.

6 At the end, go through a metal gate and across a wooden bridge and across a park. Continue down the right-hand side of the recreation ground and to the right of the dog waste bin, find a path behind the bench. The Thornhill & Sandhills Park and Ride is on your right.

7 Come out at the A40 and descend into the underpass under the road. On the other side, turn right and immediately left up Merewood Avenue and then right into Delbush Avenue.

8 At the end of Delbush Avenue, go through the wooden posts and turn right onto a narrow path. This is part of the Oxford Greenbelt Way. The path continues straight ahead for a short distance before veering to the left. Continue down the left-hand side of a field and at the end, cross a wooden bridge over a stream on the left.

9 Carry on, following a blue arrow sign to the right of the field.

10 At the end of the field, go through a small copse / gap in the hedge into a large field. The path here goes straight through the centre of the field, but you will need to find the continuation of the path, which is slightly to the right of where you come through the hedge. If there are crops growing, look for a gap of about 3 feet (1 metre) which continues diagonally upwards through the field.

11 Follow the path through the field and it will take you into a smaller field at the top within sight of some houses. Go to where it ends and then continue almost straight on, diagonally across the top of another field towards a thatched cottage.

12 Exit through a large gate beside the thatched Merry Cottage and come out onto Main Street in the village of Forest Hill, opposite The Old Chapel. Turn left along Main Street and continue, crossing the entrance to Badgers Close, to the end of the road, where you see The White Horse pub ahead.

13 Turn right onto Wheatley Road, cross the entrance to Milton Crescent and turn right up Powell Close. Go to the end of Powell Close and between house numbers 4 and 5 on the left, turn left into the narrow entrance of a footpath.

14 Cross a wooden bridge and continue along the left-hand side of the field between a hedge on the left and a fence on the right. Continue through a metal kissing gate along the left-hand side of the field. At the end of the field, go through another metal kissing gate (hidden from the other side by a huge blackberry bush) and continue straight on along the left side of the field until you get to a wooden kissing gate. Go straight on through a metal gate about 3 yards (2.7 metres) away into a wood and continue up some steps to the road.

15 Turn right and almost immediately cross the road and go left down a path to the right of a large metal field gate. Follow the green-and-yellow footpath sign and go through a small metal kissing gate. Turn right and head down the right-hand side of the field until you draw level with the start of the wood on your left. At this point, turn diagonally left down a path through the brush until you reach the edge of the wood and continue with the fence on your left. Pass under an electricity pole and continue down a narrow path until you reach a red painted wooden gate.

16 Go through the gate and straight on, crossing a track ahead of you and continuing straight ahead on the path behind the shed. Emerge into a field and walk along the left-hand side, crossing two stiles in the centre, whilst keeping the hedge to your left. Head straight on into the woods, cross a steam and a wooden stile and emerge onto a raised track.

17 Turn left along the track and then almost immediately right up a path taking you across the centre of the field. At a wide tarmac track, turn right, following the footpath sign. Pass a house called Lyehill on your right and come out on to the road in Holton.

18 Turn right and continue along the road, which is unpaved for 100 yards (91 metres), so take care. The road curves to the left (pavement to the right) and then round to the right. Follow the road over the road bridge and across the A40 road.

19 Go straight over the mini-roundabout onto Holloway Road. Just after the children's playground and the large stone dovecot, turn left into Church Road and back to the car park.

AZ walk twelve

Two Thousand Years of History

The rural village of Garsington.

This walk takes you on a healthy jaunt around the fields close to the village of Garsington, 6 miles (9.7 km) southeast of Oxford. There are some good views over the surrounding countryside and you will walk along a short section of Roman Road and past a modern electricity station as you approach what is, both physically and metaphorically, the high point of the walk. This is St Mary's Church, from where you can enjoy spectacular views of the surrounding countryside in at least three directions. Although parts of the church date back as far as the 12th century, 19th century alterations have added a pleasing set of stone angel carvings, each carrying a shield with a different symbol.

The church also has an Eric Gill memorial to Lady Ottoline Morrell who lived in Garsington Manor in the early 20th century and was often visited by well-known writers, artists and philosophers, her friends from the Bloomsbury Group. You can catch a glimpse of Garsington Manor if you make a short detour after the church. Unfortunately, it is not open to the public.

The road back passes an interesting monument, a medieval preaching cross, which once designated a preaching place in the village, and a hill imaginatively named 'The Hill'. Refreshments are available from the village's only pub, or the store in Elm Drive, opposite Kiln Lane.

start / finish	Kiln Lane, Garsington (at the junction with Oxford Road)
nearest postcode	OX44 9AR
distance	3½ miles / 5.6 km
time	2 hours
terrain	This walk is mainly dry, but could get muddy, so wear appropriate footwear. There are two stiles to cross.

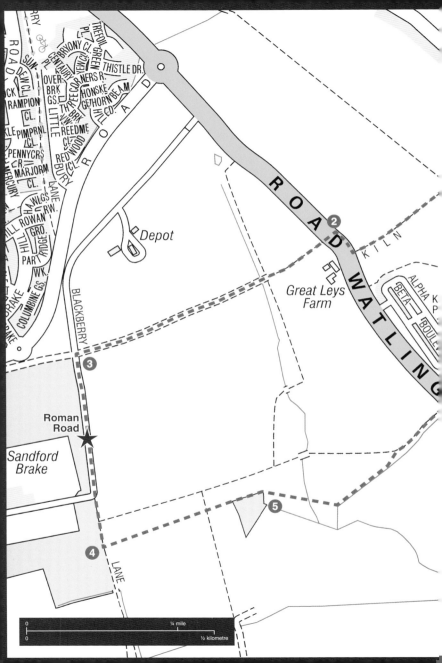

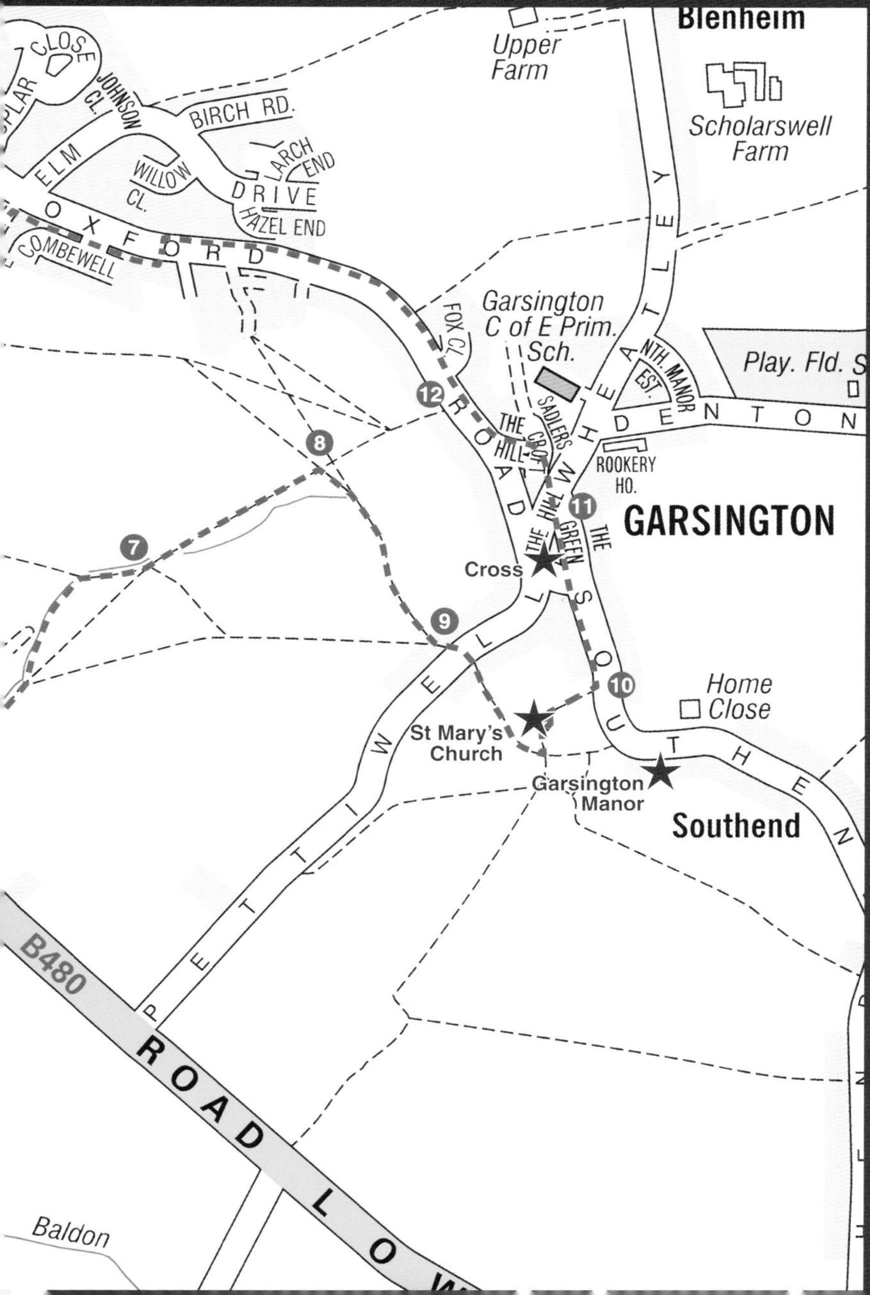

Blenheim
Upper Farm
Scholarswell Farm
POPLAR CLOSE
JOHNSON CL.
BIRCH RD.
ELM
WILLOW CL.
LARCH END
DRIVE
HAZEL END
OXFORD ROAD
COMBEWELL
FOX CL.
Garsington C of E Prim. Sch.
NTH. MANOR EST.
Play. Fld.
DENTON
THE HILL
THE CROFT
SADLERS
WHEATLEY
ROOKERY HO.
GARSINGTON
THE HILL
THE GREEN
Cross
PETTIWELL
SOUTHEND
St Mary's Church
Home Close
Garsington Manor
Southend
B480
ROAD
Baldon
12
8
11
7
9
10

There is on-street parking near the start of the walk, alternatively the village can be reached by bus from the centre of Oxford, which takes about 30 minutes. Alight just after you reach the outskirts of the village.

1 Start at Kiln Lane and go straight down it, following the blue arrow sign past Kiln Farm to the bridlepath. At the end of the bridlepath, opposite Great Leys Farm, turn right along Watlington Road.

2 Continue for about 50 yards (47 metres) and then cross the road and find a bridleway signposted 'Toot Baldon 1½ miles' through a metal gate. Go straight on across the centre of the field and then continue straight ahead down the left-hand side of the next field towards the electricity pylons.

3 At the end of the field, turn left onto a tarmac road, which runs alongside woodland behind which the electricity substation gradually becomes clearer. This is an old Roman Road ★ . At the end of the road past the substation, continue onto the path ahead.

4 At the left turn marked by a wooden post with a footpath sign on it, leave the bridleway and turn left down the footpath. Go straight ahead, passing very close to the pylon on the left and continue along the left-hand side of the field, admiring the views to the right. At the end of the field, continue straight on across planks and through a wood, then cross a wooden bridge and go straight ahead into a field.

5 You can either walk straight ahead through the field or go round the edge of the field to the right, but make sure you exit opposite where you entered. Continue straight ahead along the right-hand side of the next field. Exit the field via a kissing gate and cross a wooden bridge and immediately cross back over Watlington Road onto a concrete track opposite.

6 Just before the track is barred, turn right through a metal kissing gate onto a footpath. Walk up the left-hand side of the next field, through another metal kissing gate and continue up the left-hand side of the next field also.

7 At a crossing of paths and a break in the hedge, go left through the break which also crosses a stream (you should be able to hear the water if you can't see it) and continue up the right-hand side of the next field.

8 At a break in the hedge on the right with a footpath symbol, follow the footpath to the right and back across the stream, then diagonally across the field ahead of you to a stile. Cross the stile and go straight on up across the field, admiring the views. Cross the next stile and go straight ahead along the left-hand side of the next field, exiting between The Malthouse and Knoll House.

9 Cross Pettiwell (the continuation of Oxford Road) and take the footpath up the steps opposite marked 'To the church'. Go straight on through a wooden kissing gate and up the steps at the end to the 12th-century St Mary's Church ★ . Go right to sit on the benches behind the church to admire a superb panoramic view across Oxfordshire. Continue going anticlockwise round the church following the gravel path and continue past the graveyard, exiting through the church gate.

10 For the detour to view Garsington Manor ★ , turn right and walk a short distance along Southend Road. Otherwise, turn left past the thatched Stone House and continue along the road.

11 Just past the medieval preaching cross ★ on your left and opposite the war memorial, you come to a T junction. Cross over and go down a narrow street with a barrier across it called 'The Hill'. At the bottom of The Hill, turn right and continue upwards along a path which is elevated above Oxford Road.

12 Cross Fox Close and continue straight on. The road will then go downwards. Keep going and eventually reach a red house opposite metal barriers in front of a path. Cross over and take this path along the backs of the houses, crossing Combewell, with a hedge on the right-hand side. Arrive back at Kiln Lane.

AZ walk thirteen

The Mysterious Folly

Hurst Hill and Youlbury Wood.

This walk starts 3 miles (4.8 km) to the west of Oxford city centre, on a path that is conveniently hidden behind a bus stop on Cumnor Hill. It takes you along a narrow but well-frequented path between sports fields and up onto Hurst Hill, which promises a folly but delivers a trig point. The leafy walk is enjoyable as well as good uphill exercise and takes you twice through a field of very friendly sheep if you go at the right time of year.

You then explore another tree-covered area at Youlbury Wood, home to the sprawling Youlbury Scout Activity Centre and a Carmelite Priory, where you can attend Mass with the discalced friars, should you so wish. The return journey offers some breathtaking views of Oxford and also crosses Oxford Brookes University's Harcourt Hill Campus, where you can admire some smart new student accommodation and a view of their generous sports facilities. A quick tour of a modern housing estate brings you out within yards of the original bus stop.

start / finish	Lime Road bus stop, North Hinksey
nearest postcode	OX2 9EH
distance	5½ miles / 8.8 km
time	3 hours
terrain	Mostly footpaths, which can get very muddy. Two ascents.

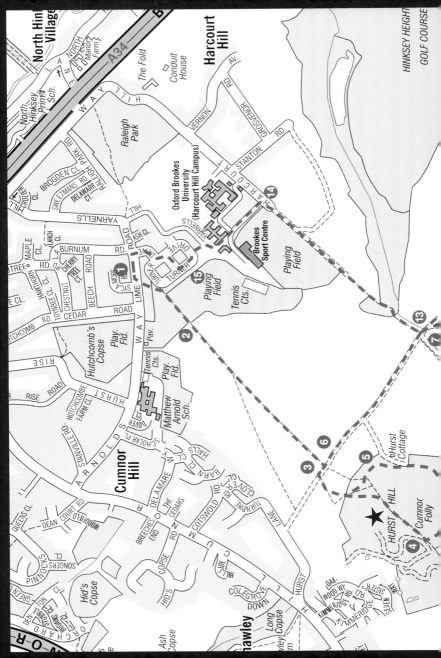

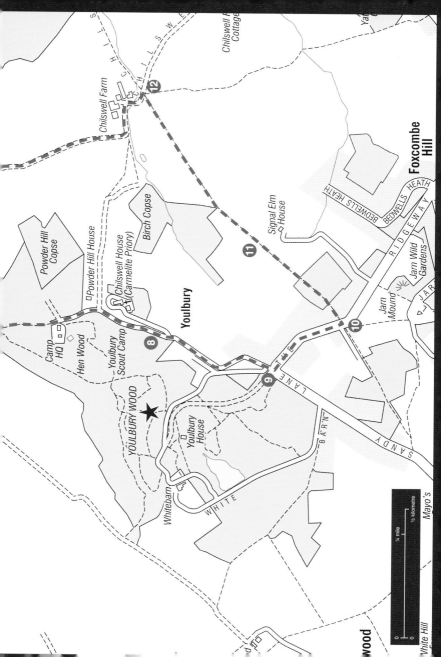

The walk starts at Lime Road bus stop, between Sycamore Road and Laburnum Road, which is served by buses from the city centre. Parking is available at Louie Memorial Fields on Arnolds Way, which is a continuation of Lime Road.

1 Behind the bus stop is a narrow path which disappears to the right into woodland, at the entrance to which you will find a sign marked 'Bridleway Chawley 1'. Follow this path straight on, ignoring the paths which cross it from left to right at a couple of points. It will take you between playing fields and continues for about 10 minutes until there is a 3-way fork ahead of you. Take the central fork almost straight ahead but slightly to the right, marked 'Bridleway Westminster College'. This will take you between a large number of blackberry bushes and continues forward to some wide, gravelled steps taking you gently upwards.

2 At the next fork, stay on the main path to the right (not through the wood to the left). You will continue along the right-hand side of a field and go uphill. At the oak tree in the centre of the field, pause to admire the views. You will find an inaccessible watching post just after the tree. You will then descend the field, spotting Farmoor Reservoir in the distance on your right.

3 At the bottom of the field, pass through a gap in the hedge and then go right onto a wide track and left through a kissing gate about 25 yards (23 metres) further on. Go straight on up the path ahead towards the wood. Go through two metal gates and you will be on Hurst Hill ★ . Go straight on up the hill. You will come to a clearing and find a concrete trig point to the left ahead of you. Despite the name on the map, there is no obvious folly.

4 Continue straight on up the path to the right of the trig point and then turn left through the wood, taking the left fork until you are in a wooded area with no discernible marked path. You just need to continue left, but keep to the right-hand side of the wood and with the fields on your right. Eventually you will find a clearly marked path at the border of the wood with the field.

5 Follow the path downwards to more brush through the wooded area. Eventually the path will go along a fence, which will be on your right-hand side. Return to the gate where you entered the wood and exit both gates back to the field and retrace your steps across the field to the track.

6 Turn right along the track and continue straight across a crossroads with a farm to the left.

7 At the next crossroads, go straight on and then take a path to the right across the field and go through a gate into Youlbury Wood ★ . Go straight up the track, passing Gate 4 to the Youlbury Scout Activity Centre on the right and later Powder Hill House on your left. Keep going straight on, past a wooden hut on the left.

8 Just past Gate 3 of the Scout camp, turn right at a T junction (see sign to Carmelite Priory on your left). Continue past Boars Hill Reservoir on the left and Picketts Heath Barn.

9 At the T junction follow the sign marked 'Oxford' left opposite Youlbury Lodge. This is Sandy Lane. Follow Sandy Lane as it turns to the right and becomes a track called The Ridgeway.

10 When you come to a postbox on the left opposite Hunter's Chase, follow the Bridleway marked 'Chilswell Farm ¾ mile'. Don't turn down the drive of The Haltings by mistake – the bridleway entrance is to the right and it is tiny. Continue down the bridleway, along the backs of houses to the right and then a garden fence. It plunges downwards into woodland and then rises.

11 At the end, go through a metal gate and admire a great view of Oxford and its surrounding hills. Follow the path straight on across the field and downwards. Pass a big, round, concrete cattle trough and exit through a gate just beyond it.

12 Go to the left, signposted 'Bridleway', which goes left under some trees. Continue along the track, which bends to the right past a barn and through a gate. This is Chilswell Farm. Continue until the next gate, following the Oxford Green Belt Way for just over ¾ mile (1.2 km).

13 At the end of the sheep field, turn right down a narrow path opposite the gate. At the wood, take the left fork and go upwards. Pass an electricity substation on the left and go straight on.

14 Where the path reaches a road, turn left through Oxford Brookes University, with the playing fields on your left and buildings to your right. Continue past Westminster Hall and through a park with a children's play area on the right.

15 Enter the housing estate on Ruskin Close, turn first right into Turner Drive, then first left, then first right. Arrive back at Lime Road and turn left, back to the bus stop.

A-Z walk fourteen

Woodland and Riverside

Radley Woods and the River Thames.

Situated south of Oxford, 5 miles (8 km) from the city centre, Radley village has ancient roots, dating as far back as the Neolithic era, and a church founded in around 1300. Today it is best known for its public school, Radley College, which occupies a large area of land at the western end of the village.

This walk will take you from the railway station (Radley is conveniently the first stop after Oxford on the train!) up to Radley Little and Large Woods, with views over Radley College's playing fields. The woods are particularly beautiful in late April and early May as they are carpeted in bluebells. On leaving the woods, you will turn down towards the village of Kennington and meet the river along the Thames Path at Sandford Lock. Back in Lower Radley, look out for some striking thatched cottages, some dating back to the 16th century.

There are pubs at Sandford Lock and near the start/finish point where you can stop for refreshments.

start / finish	Radley Railway Station
nearest postcode	OX14 3BJ
distance	5 miles / 8 km
time	2 hours
terrain	A mixture of pavements and compacted woodland and riverside paths, which can get muddy. One stile to cross.

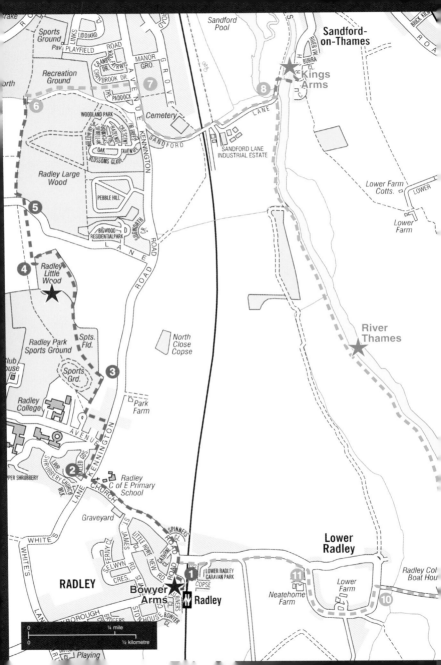

The walk starts in the car park in front of Radley train station. You could park here, arrive by train from Oxford to Radley, or else take the bus from Oxford or Abingdon to Radley Station.

1 Head out of the car park and turn right into Foxborough Road. Follow this round to the left after the Village Shop, where it becomes Church Road and keep going straight on. You will eventually pass a graveyard to your left and a few minutes later Radley C of E Primary School and Radley Church on your right. Head towards Radley College.

2 Turn right and cross Kennington Road, taking the path along the fence of Radley College, which is increasingly raised above the road. Pass the front gates of Radley College ★ and continue past the bus stop until you find a kissing gate signed 'Kennington 1½ miles'. Turn left through the gate and go straight on following the path. This takes you past some of the houses provided for staff at the school and turns right just before one of the boys' houses. You will then pass a green space with a sports pavilion on the left and a couple more college houses on the right.

3 Keep going until you find a public footpath sign, and follow the narrow path to the left alongside a stream. This takes you past the playing fields all the way to Radley Little Wood ★. Carry straight on, across a small stream, until you meet a fork in the path. Take the right-hand fork for a picturesque circular walk of the wood. In late April and early May this is a carpet of bluebells.

4 Once you have followed the circular walk for some time, you will meet a signpost marked 'Public Footpath' indicated in two directions. Take the right-hand path. Go through the gateposts to your right and turn immediately right along a path between a fence and a Radley College playing field. Keep going and you will come out at a field. Carry straight on, crossing the field until you get to Sugworth Lane.

5 Cross Sugworth Lane, climb over the stile and enter Radley Large Wood ★. Take the left-hand footpath and carry straight on along the side of the wood. You will have views of fields to the left. Eventually you will get to a bridge.

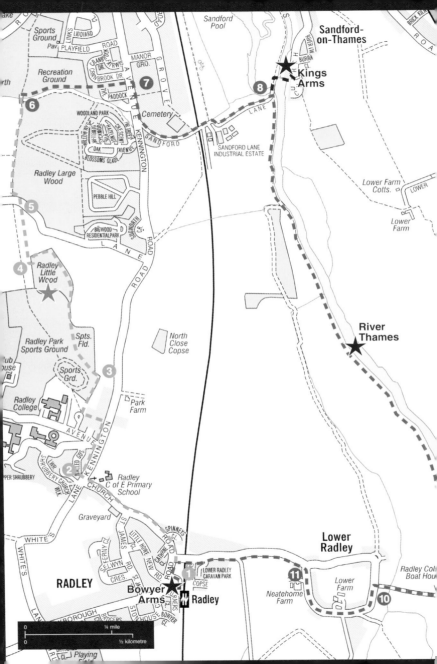

6 Cross the bridge and find the gate afterwards. Go through the gate and turn immediately right across an area of recreation ground. You will find there is a stream on your right. The green space will narrow and you will find you are walking behind some houses. Keep going straight on. There may be cows in the field in front of you. At the end of the field, you will see a gate on your left. Go through the gate, which brings you out onto The Avenue in the village of Kennington.

7 Cross The Avenue and turn right, then go immediately left down Sandford Lane, where you see a sign indicating 'Sandford Lane Industrial Estate and Cemetery'. Go past St Swithun's churchyard, under the railway bridge and past Kennington Meadows. Pass Sandford Lane Industrial Estate on your right. The road goes round to right and then left. Take the elevated path to avoid walking in the road.

8 Arrive at Sandford Lock bridge. If you wish to visit The Kings Arms ★ in nearby Sandford-on-Thames, cross over the bridge in front of you, turn left and cross over the lock. The pub is visible on the left. Return to the bridge to continue the walk. Otherwise, at the end of Sandford Lane turn right onto the Thames Path in the direction of 'Lower Radley 1½ miles' as indicated on the sign. You will now walk along some beautiful stretches of the River Thames ★, which will be on your left.

9 Continue along the Thames Path for 1½ miles (2.4 km) until you reach a gate leading to a bridge to the side of the Radley College Boat House. Cross over the bridge and once past the boathouse and the house beside it, take the road up to Lower Radley.

10 At the T junction, turn left and follow the road, which will turn right and pass an ancient barn and some thatched cottages on the right, the second one of which dates to 1513 – see if you can see the inscription on the wall. The road is a loop and when you have covered three sides of the loop, a road will go off to the left.

11 Take this road to the left. You will pass several fields until you reach more houses. Keep going, cross the railway bridge beside Radley Station and turn left on Foxborough Road to return to your train, car or the bus stop or to pop into the Bowyer Arms ★ for some refreshment.

⒜⒵ walk fifteen

England's Oldest Town

Abingdon-on-Thames.

Abingdon is believed to be England's oldest continuously inhabited town and lies on the River Thames 7 miles (11.3 km) south of Oxford. It boasted an abbey as far back as the 7th century and on this walk you can still see the ruins of Abingdon Abbey, dating from the time of King Henry VIII's Dissolution of the Monasteries in 1538. The Abbey Gardens are well kept and their circular flower beds are particularly lovely in spring and summer.

Any visit to Abingdon should feature the river and on this walk you will cross over the weir leading to Abingdon Lock, built in 1790, and walk along the Thames. This walk is particularly delightful in summer, when the river is lined with canal and pleasure boats. Further on, you will encounter the end of the Wilts & Berks Canal, which made Abingdon an important transport link between London, Birmingham and Bristol.

The town itself is small but picturesque, with the medieval St Helen's Church and its adjoining almshouses adding interest and historical flavour to the walk. In the town centre, the magnificent Abingdon County Hall towers over the main square and houses an impressive museum for a town of this size. Buns are still traditionally thrown from its roof on special occasions. There are several cafés on Abingdon Town Square and the Nag's Head on Abingdon Bridge provides both refreshments and views.

start / finish	Cattle Market Car Park, Abbey Close
nearest postcode	OX14 3HL
distance	3 miles / 4.8 km
time	1 hour 30 minutes
terrain	Mostly paved, with some parkland and potentially muddy riverbanks. Some steps to climb.

ST.
ST. MARY'S GRN.
ST. NICHOLAS'
GREEN
WOOD CL.
HERON'S WLK.
HARCOURT
WHITELOCK
BRO...
HAM
RD.
CLEVELAND
NORMAN
Prim. Sch.
LAMMAS CL.
ORCHARD CL.

DARRELL
STANILAND CT.
MARSH
RFIELD PL.
ROAD
JOHN MASON
RD.
WARWICK CL.
SWINBURNE
GALL...
GALL...
FLD.
F...
FD.

FIN-
MORE
CL.
ST.
St. Nicolas
C of E Prim.
Sch.
ENHALL RD.
BOWYER
GEOFFREY BARBOUR RD.
RD.
FOUNTAIN CT.
CONV.
WARREN

XHILL
WALK
BOXHILL
Rec. Grd.
RD.
Conv.
Schs.
Ten. Cts. A
St. Edmund's
Catholic
Prim. Sch.
THE
LEE
DUNDAS CL.
AV.

W...
NEWHAM SQ.
FITZHARRY'S RD.
CLIFTON DR.
ABBOTT
THESYGER
RD.
THE
HOLT
Rec.
Grd.
FARRIERS
M.
JACKMAN CL.
SHERWOOD
CURTIS
CRABTREE PL.
E...

ST.
LETCOMBE AV.
FORD DR.
KINGSTON CL.
RD.
Playgrd.
AV.

B4017 BATH ST.
55
FITZHARRY
STN.
T.H.
MOTTE
WITHINGTON CT.
NEWS CT.
QUAKER'S CT.
PENLON PL.
THAMES CT.
VIEW
Works

STRATTON
WAY
VINEYARD
OXFORD A4183
13
STERT ST.
OLD STA. YD.
ABBEY
Super-market
BURGESS
Abingdon
Abbey
Gds.
Abbey
Stream
Play
Area
Abbey
Meadows
3

B4017 ST.
Lib.
BROAD
THE
CHARTER
BURY ST.
ON ST.
MKT.
CHCH.
COUNCIL
Offs.
CLOSE
THAMES
Ab...

STREET HIGH S
Town
Square
Mus.
BATH
ST. HELEN'S
LOMB...
ST.
TURNAGAIN
BRIDGE
CHURCH WLK.
Thtre.
Swim.
Pool
Rye
Farm Meadow

COOPERS
CT.
WEAVER
ST.
S.EM'S
LA.
FAIRLAWN
WHARF
The Old Gaol
The
Cosener's Ho.
ABINGDON-ON-
THAMES
Rye
Farm

...TER.
MILL
GNET
STREAM
CT.
9
ST. HELEN'S
CT.
ST.
WEST ST. HELEN ST.
Maud
Hales
Bri.

MANOR
CT.
St. Helen's
Church
ST. HELEN'S CHURCHYARD
Hales
Meadow
Pav.
Club

ROAD
PADDOCK
7
WILSHAM
ST. HELEN'S
Playing
Field
Abingdon
Town FC
ANDERSEY
ISLAND

WHARF
CL.
FERRY
WLK.
8
RIVER THA...
CULHAM
A415

MORRIS
RD.
ROAD

0   ¼ mile
0   ½ kilometre

1
2
4
5
6
10
11

Abingdon can be reached by bus from Oxford. Otherwise, there are several car parks in the town.

1 Start in the Cattle Market car park. Go through the gate marked 'Welcome to Abbey Gardens'. In front of you will be a circle of flowerbeds. Turn left and head along a short path to a second part of the park with a statue of Queen Victoria on your left and the ruins of Abingdon Abbey ★ on your right. Follow the path diagonally across the park and exit just before a steel-topped cone to your left and cross the bridge in front of you.

2 Turn immediately left before the lido, so that you have a stream on your left and toilets on your right. Continue along the path, past a large children's playground on your right. Continue for some time until you reach the weir on the River Thames. Follow the path over the weir, which will take you to Abingdon Lock ★ .

3 Cross the lock and turn right. Follow the path along the riverside until you reach Abingdon's stone bridge.

4 You have the option here to continue under the bridge along the riverside path as far as you fancy. There should be several canal boats moored alongside and there is a good view

across the river towards Abingdon town centre and St Helen's Church ★ . Turn back and retrace your steps under the stone bridge. Go up the steps to the road and turn right to cross the bridge towards Abingdon town centre. Stop at The Nag's Head for refreshment if required.

5 Cross Bridge Street at the crossing opposite the Old Gaol. Pass Turnagain Lane and just after Abingdon City Hall on the right but before Abingdon County Hall ahead of you, turn left down East St Helen's Street. Pass the Kings Head & Bell on your left and the 15th Century House and Unicorn House with its blue plaque commemorating the visit of King William III.

6 At the end of the road, cross over and go under the stone arch immediately opposite, to the right of St Helen's Church. When you find Twitty's Almshouses on your right, turn left so that you walk between the church and the Long Alley Almshouses. On reaching St Helen's Wharf, turn right. You should have the river to your left. Pass the Old Anchor Inn on your right and continue to the bridge with white railings where the Wilts & Berks Canal meets the Thames. Cross the bridge and continue straight on.

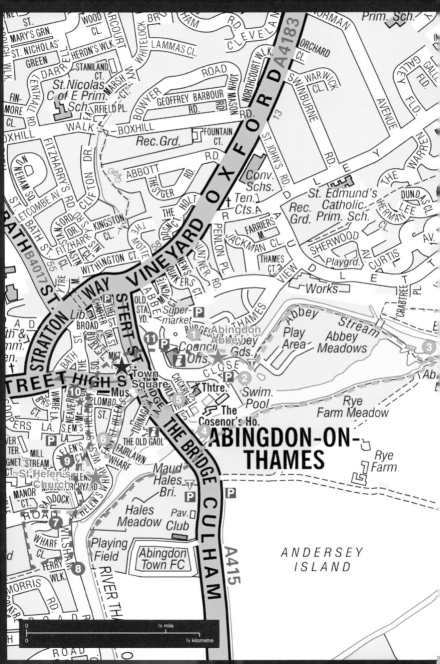

7 Cross Mill Paddock and continue along the footpath with the hedge on the left. After about 20 yards (18 metres), you will find an entrance to the left. Turn left through this entrance and walk down the left-hand side of the recreation ground. Continue through the car park and turn left onto Ferry Walk.

8 At the end of Ferry Walk, turn left past the Old Foundry and continue along the riverbank. Cross back over the bridge with the white railings again and turn sharp left along the private road alongside the canal.

9 At St Helen's Mill, where the road ends, turn right and walk alongside the cemetery and Twitty's Almshouses, to your left. Go back through the stone arch, with St Helen's Church on your right this time. Then turn left down West St Helen's Street.

10 At the end of West St Helen's Street, cross the High Street at the crossing and turn right. When you reach Abingdon County Hall Museum, turn left into the Town Square ★ . There are places you can stop for refreshments here, otherwise exit the square via the small alley diagonally opposite where you entered it and emerge onto Stert Street. Cross at the pedestrian crossing opposite you and go straight on down the narrow drive ahead of you to the right.

11 At the end, cross over Abbey Close and continue straight on, on the path to the right of Abbey House. At the end, turn right down a path with red railings either side and then left, back into Abbey Gardens. Finally, turn left out of Abbey Gardens back into the Cattle Market car park.

A̅Z̅ walk sixteen

Countryside Rambles

Pinsley Wood and Church Hanborough.

The lovely village of Church Hanborough is 9 miles (14.5 km) northwest of Oxford in the rolling Oxfordshire countryside. There are three options for walking here, all starting at the 900-year-old church. The full walk takes in an hour-long circuit of Pinsley Wood followed by a longer loop around open countryside. For shorter options you could choose to follow either one of these individual circuits.

Pinsley Wood is owned by the Blenheim estate but has a public footpath around its perimeter. Beware: the path is slippery when muddy, and very uneven as it is riddled with tree roots, so it is only suitable for the surefooted. But if you go in spring, it is a beautiful sea of bluebells.

The second, longer leg of the walk takes you through some very pleasant countryside, where you can encounter cows, sheep and wildflower meadows as well as a variety of agricultural crops and, in autumn, some very good blackberrying opportunities.

The walk instructions described here are for the full walk. For the shorter Pinsley Wood walk, follow steps 1 to 3, and for the longer countryside loop only, start at step 4.

start / finish	St Peter & St Paul Church, Church Hanborough
nearest postcode	OX29 8AB
distance	Full walk – 6½ miles / 9.7 km
	Pinsley Wood walk – 2 miles / 3.2 km
	Countryside walk – 4½ miles / 7.2 km
time	3 hours, 1 hour or 2 hours
terrain	This walk can get muddy, particularly in the wood, where there are also tree roots across the path. There are eight stiles to cross.

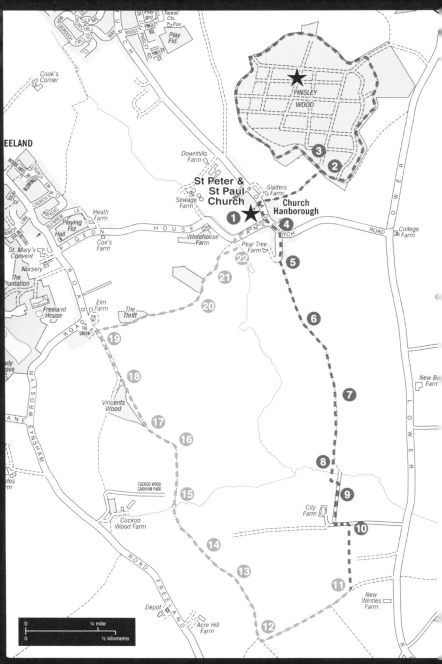

1 Start at the car park in front of St Peter & St Paul Church ★ in Church Hanborough. Cross the road and go up the footpath to the left of the Hand & Shears pub. The footpath narrows between a field and a thatched cottage; keep going and after almost 10 minutes, enter Pinsley Wood ★ between two wooden posts.

2 Turn right along the path and stay on the same path as you complete an anticlockwise circuit around the perimeter of the wood. Ignore three exits from the wood, and where the perimeter fence starts to distance itself from the path, stay on the path. You will pass a stand of pines to your right and the path will then meet a barbed wire fence and a gate into the pine stand. Keep following the perimeter path.

3 Look out on your right for the wooden posts where you entered, with the orange footpath arrow sign and a hand-painted sign directing you to the Hand & Shears pub. Turn right to go back up the path and retrace your steps to the village. Turn left at the road to return to the church.

4 To continue with the countryside walk, go past the church. If you are starting your walk here, turn right out of the church car park. Continue along Church Lane until you reach the second road on the right, opposite Walnut Cottage, where you will see a sign to a footpath marked 'Eynsham 2½'. Turn right to follow the direction of the sign.

5 At the end of the lane, go through a metal kissing gate marked with an orange footpath sign and follow the path along a hedge to your left.

6 At the fork with a barn to the right, go straight on (left fork) and continue through a gate and down the left-hand side of a large field with a hedge to your left.

7 At the bottom of the field, go through a kissing gate and straight ahead across a field towards a fence on the left along which the path continues.

8 At the bottom of the field, continue straight across a track and a brook and exit through a metal kissing gate. Turn left along the path and at a raised ridge in the centre of the small field, turn right across the field and exit through a kissing gate to the right of a large wooden gate.

9 Go straight on up the farm track, past City Farm and houses. At the T junction, turn left along the road.

10 About 100 yards (91 metres) further on, find a metal kissing gate on the right and turn right into the field, continuing along the left-hand side of the field. At the end, cross a track with a works entrance on your right. Go straight on alongside a steep embankment full of blackberry bushes on the right.

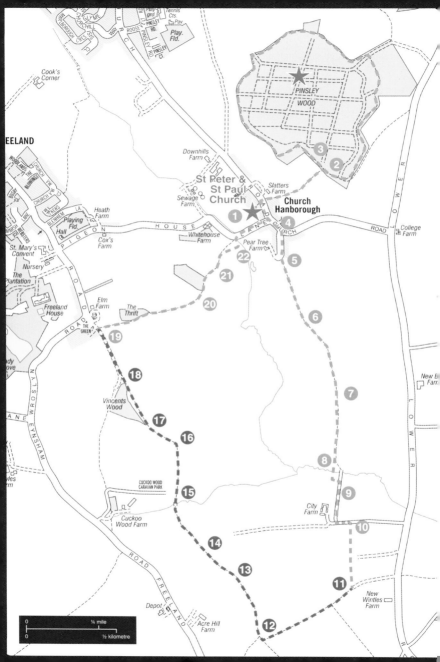

11 At the next gate, turn right along the bridleway towards the fields, with the bushes and trees now on your right. Go straight on through the gap beside a large metal gate and continue to another gate into an open field. Go to the right along the bridleway between bushes (this part can be very prickly!). You will eventually come out into a large field, but the path plunges back between hedges to the right-hand side.

12 At the end, where there is a T junction of paths, turn right and go straight on, ignoring the left turn, to a stile ahead of you. Cross the stile into a field and continue across the top of the field over another stile and continue straight on along the left-hand side of the next field, with a hedge on your left.

13 At the end of this field, find a double stile. Cross both stiles and go left across the field with a fence on your right. Find the next stile behind an oak tree and continue straight on along the right-hand edge of the next field. You will see a farm in the distance to the left.

14 At the end of the field, cross the next stile and a small wooden bridge into woodland. Emerge about 10 yards (9 metres) on into a field and follow the path straight on along the right-hand side of the field.

15 At the end of the field, go through a wooded area and emerge across a wooden bridge across a stream and through a metal gate. Follow the path on the left-hand side of the field and then go through a wooden kissing gate left of a large wooden gate and go up the left-hand side of the next field.

16 At the end of the field turn left following the path through blackberry bushes and find another wooden kissing gate. Continue on the left-hand side of the field.

17 At the end of the field by the dead tree, go through another wooden kissing gate. Do not go up the small path to the left, but keep straight on, through a dense brush and wooded area.

18 At the end of the wood, go through a wooden kissing gate to a large field and continue straight on to the left-hand side of the field. At the end of the field, you will see a house with an arched window ahead of you. Turn left before it through a wooden kissing gate, following a footpath sign and turn right up the track.

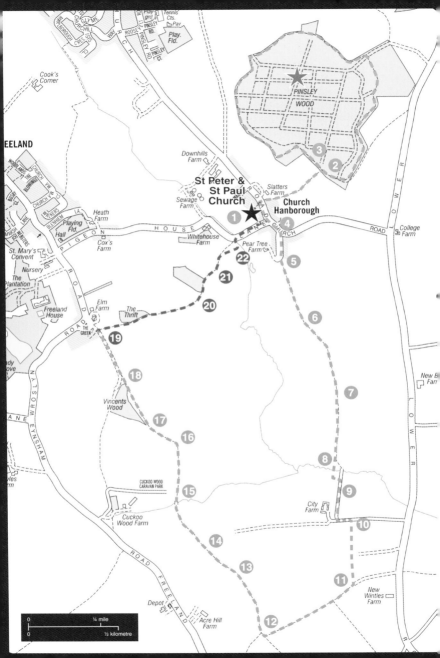

19 At Glebe Farm (see the large stone sign to the right), turn right following the footpath marked 'Church Hanborough ½'. Go through the black gate to the right of Elm Farm and continue straight on down the left-hand side of the field. Go through a wooden gate and straight on up the left-hand side of the field.

20 At the end of the field, turn left over the stile, where you will find a wooden bridge and a further stile. Follow the path diagonally across the field to the wooden gate opposite.

21 Go through the gate, turn right and cross to a gate on the right. Go through the gate and across a bridge and diagonally across the field in the direction of the church spire.

22 Pass through a ramshackle gate and turn left down a track. At the end, turn right along a shaded road, Pigeon House Lane, and climb upwards to a T junction with 'Thatched Cottage' (Post Office Stores) ahead. Turn left onto Church Road and return to the church car park.

AZ walk seventeen

Victory Parade

Woodstock and Blenheim Park.

Twelve miles (19.3 km) north of Oxford, the town of Woodstock grew up to service the requirements of the royal visitors to Woodstock Palace. Originally built as a hunting lodge by King Henry I in the 12th century and embellished by his grandson Henry II, the palace was sadly destroyed during the English Civil War. In the 18th century, however, a new and altogether more magnificent palace was built: Blenheim, the seat of the Dukes of Marlborough to the present day, gifted to the original duke by Queen Anne and a grateful nation following the Battle of Blenheim.

This walk provides a superb view of the Column of Victory – atop which stands a statue of the first Duke of Marlborough, dressed as a triumphant Roman emperor – as well as of the palace itself. There is a fee for entering the palace and its immediate grounds, but this walk takes public footpaths through the Blenheim estate, through areas which are free to visit.

Returning to Woodstock, you climb some challenging steps and alight in the centre of town, passing the Museum of Oxfordshire, with its stocks, and enjoying a good view of its historic Town Hall. There is a choice of pubs and eateries to refuel in after the walk, including an excellent deli on Oxford Road.

start / finish	Union Street Car Park, off Hensington Road, Woodstock
nearest postcode	OX20 1JF
distance	5½ miles / 8.8 km
time	2 hours 30 minutes
terrain	Mostly pavements and good paths, though some parts can get muddy. There are a lot of steps to climb.

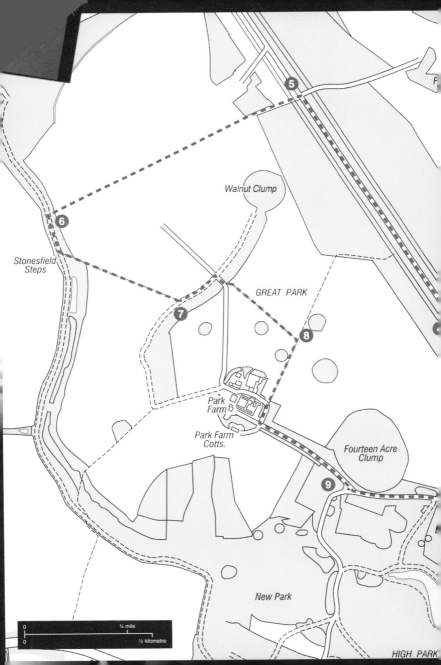

Walnut Clump

Stonesfield
Steps

GREAT PARK

Park
Farm

Park Farm
Cotts.

Fourteen Acre
Clump

New Park

HIGH PARK

| 0 | | ¼ mile |
| 0 | | ½ kilometre |

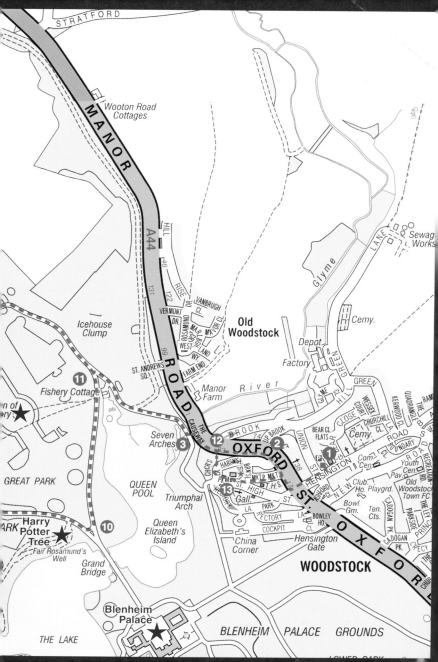

Woodstock is served by various buses from Oxford city centre. Alternatively there is parking in Union Street car park.

1 From the car park entrance on Hensington Road, turn right past the fire station and walk to the junction with Oxford Street. Turn right and cross over at the pedestrian crossing, continuing right on the other side of the road.

2 Follow Oxford Street as it bends to the left and divides into two parts. Continue along the path on the upper, left-hand, part and at a fork with a sign warning of 'Overhanging Building', turn right down a flight of steps onto the lower road. At the bottom of the steps, turn left and continue along Oxford Street as it bends to the right. Pass a row of small houses and, in sight of The Black Prince pub, you come to a green gate directly ahead of you on the left-hand pavement.

3 Go through the green gate, down a short alley and then through a subsequent green gate on the left. You will now be in Blenheim Park ★ at the Seven Arches Bridge. Turn right and follow the wide tarmac path which will take you past the lake and give you a view of Blenheim Palace ★ in the distance. Go round to the right past a derelict cottage. At the fork in the road, continue straight on along the right-hand fork.

4 Continue straight on along Wychwood Way. This is a very long path, between rows of trees. Look backwards after some minutes to see a view of the Column of Victory ★ and Blenheim Palace in the distance. Eventually you will cross a cattle grid between a line of fences. Continue almost to the second line of fences and second cattle grid and just before it, turn left along the public footpath.

5 You will pass woods on your right. Continue straight on and join a track at the end of the woodland, heading straight ahead. Eventually head through a wooden gate, across a tarmac road, through another wooden gate and go straight on across a large field toward distant woodland. Go through the gate into the wood and follow the path straight on until you meet a crossroad with a high stone wall in front of you.

6 Turn left along the path and continue almost until you reach a sign marked 'Private'. At this point, turn left and cross a bridge with wooden railings. This is 'Shakespeare's Way'. Continue straight on and out of the wood. The path takes you along the right side of a field and then through a gate and across another field.

7 At the next gate, turn left and follow the track alongside more woodland. When you reach the road, turn right and continue until you have passed some trees (about 30 yards / 27 metres). You will find a sign with a map and a kissing gate to the left. Go through the kissing gate, continue across a small field to the next kissing gate and then go diagonally across a large field, staying to the right of a stand of Copper Beeches.

8 At the end of the field, go through another kissing gate and turn right along the path. You will pass Park Farm on your right and then follow the road, which bends round to the left, through the trees.

9 At the junction, keep going along the road as it bends to the left. As you approach the lake, look out for the Harry Potter tree ★ through the gate to the right, but keep straight on if you don't want to visit it.

10 Just before the Grand Bridge, turn left and go round to the left so you are almost walking back on yourself. Continue straight on until you pass the ruined cottage.

11 Turn sharp right and continue on the path until you come back to the green gate through which you entered the park. Exit through the gate and turn right and proceed past the small cottages (now on your right).

12 At the first set of steps you encounter to your right, go up the steps (quite a climb!) and emerge onto Chaucer's Lane. Go straight ahead to the end of Chaucer's Lane and then turn left onto Park Street.

13 Ahead of you is Woodstock Town Hall. Take the left fork and walk along Market Street until you reach Oxford Street. Turn right onto Oxford Street and either catch your bus or return to the car park by crossing the road and heading left down Hensington Road and left again past the fire station.

ᴀ̶z walk eighteen

Reservoir of Views

A choice of walks around Farmoor Reservoir.

Farmoor Reservoir lies 5 miles (8 km) to the west of Oxford. Considering its size – it has a capacity of up to 12 million litres of water – the reservoir is a well-kept secret. Those in the know are mainly water sports enthusiasts and birdwatchers. Once you have discovered it, the walks come as a revelation. On a sunny day, with the sailing boats and windsurfers on the water, there is a holiday feel to the place and some great views.

There are several walks to do in this area depending on how much time you have, with the option to either keep to the water's edge or take a wider circuit through the surrounding countryside.

Whichever route you take, if you are visiting during the summer you could round your walk off at Oxford Sailing Club's café, which serves tea and homemade cake with a perfect view over the water.

start / finish **nearest postcode**	Farmoor Reservoir Car Park, Cumnor Road, Farmoor OX2 9NS
RESERVOIR WALKS: **distance** **time** **terrain**	Ranging from 1¾ miles / 2.7 km to 4 miles / 6.6 km 1 hour 30 minutes for the longest walk Flat, dry, paved walkways.
COUNTRYSIDE WALK: **distance** **time** **terrain**	3½ miles / 5.6 km 1 hour 30 minutes Mostly footpaths, which can get muddy after rain.

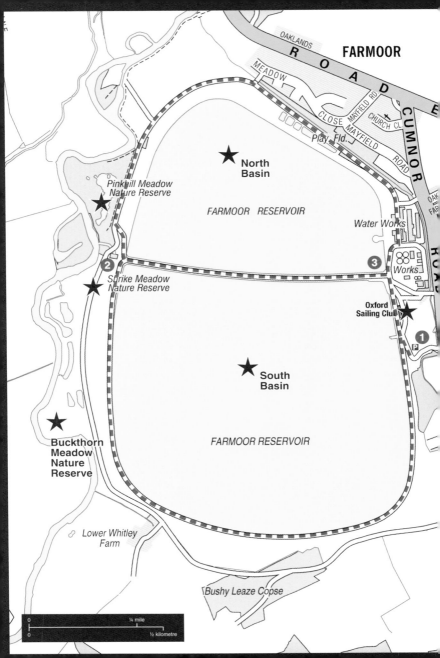

The Reservoir Walks

There are four options to choose from for walks around the reservoir's edge, so there is a walk to suit everyone.

North Basin (Farmoor 1)
1¾ miles / 2.7 km (35 minutes)

1 Start at the car park and walk up to the reservoir by way of the ramp in front of you. Turn right at the top and walk past the Oxford Sailing Club ★ . Keep going around the north end of the reservoir.

2 When you are opposite the sailing club, turn left and walk back down the central causeway, turning right at the end to return to the car park.

South Basin (Farmoor 2)
2½ miles / 4.3 km (50 minutes)

1 Start at the car park and walk up to the reservoir by way of the ramp in front of you. Turn left at the top and walk around the south end of the reservoir.

2 When you are opposite the sailing club, turn right and walk back down the central causeway, turning right at the end to return to the car park.

Reservoir Circuit
3½ miles / 5.6 km (1 hour 15 minutes)

1 Start at the car park and walk up to the reservoir by way of the ramp in front of you. Turn either left or right at the top, depending on whether you wish to walk in a clockwise or anticlockwise direction, and complete a circuit of the whole reservoir.

Figure-of-Eight
4 miles / 6.6 km (1 hour 30 minutes)

1 Start at the car park and walk up to the reservoir by way of the ramp in front of you. Turn either left or right at the top, depending on which direction you wish to walk in first, and walk around the end of the reservoir.

2 When you reach the opposite side, walk down the central causeway.

3 At the end of the walkway, turn either left or right to complete a circuit of the other basin, returning again along the central causeway and back to the start.

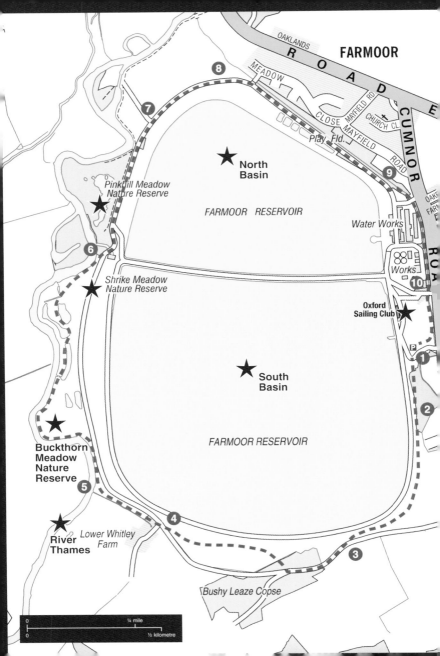

The Countryside Walk

Farmoor Reservoir also offers a Countryside Walk from the car park, along well-maintained paths, through fields and along some lovely River Thames meanders, with occasional views of the reservoir. On a hot day, this offers some shade and you can still re-join the reservoir for tea at the café. The path is well signposted, but here are some brief directions.

1 From the car park, head down the path in the left-hand corner nearest the reservoir, where the sign advertises a 'Countryside Walk'.

2 Follow the path past the toilets and you will soon have good views of the reservoir to your right and open countryside to your left. The paths goes through some small areas of woodland. When you come to the place where the path ahead is barred, look for the sign pointing left marked 'Countryside Walk'.

3 The route joins a road for a short distance until just before a fork, where you turn to the right to walk along a boardwalk.

4 Walk along a path with fences on both sides, at the end of which there is a bridge to the left with black railings. Cross the bridge, turn right onto a road and re-find the path to the right of a yellow house marked 'No.1'.

5 The path eventually leads you to the River Thames ★. When you reach a gate, continue along the river rather than going right through the gate. Continue along the river ignoring right turns.

6 Turn left onto a gravel footpath by a brick building, then cross the bridge by the sluice and continue through a gate following the signpost to 'Pinkhill Meadow car park 200 m' (rather than taking the left-hand fork).

7 Turn right at the fork in the field, in sight of some houses.

8 At a gateway, turn left along a footpath. On your right there is a low brick building surrounded by grey railings. Shortly afterwards, turn left onto a track and immediately right past the bridge, following the signpost.

9 As you reach the Treatment Works turn left and then immediately right, after which you will come to a road and to an entrance marked 'Farmoor Water Treatment Works'. Go down the narrow path following the green arrow just to the left-hand side of the entrance.

10 Continue along the path, passing the first entrance. At the second entrance, marked 'Farmoor Reservoirs', turn right back into Farmoor Reservoir car park.

ᴀ̲z̲ walk nineteen

Snake Heads and Blankets

Ducklington, Witney and Witney Lake.

The little village of Ducklington nestles to the south of the market town of Witney, 13 miles (30 km) west of Oxford. It is particularly well known for the meadow near the church where the snake's head fritillary flower grows in abundance. The meadow is open to the public one day a year – 'Fritillary Sunday' – when Morris dancers perform and cream teas are served in the church hall. The date of this event, usually in April, can be found each year on the Ducklington Village website.

The Square, where this walk starts, is the oldest part of Ducklington and boasts some picturesque, thatched cottages and a nearby country pub. However, within five minutes, you are in countryside, crossing open fields that are full of lambs in springtime.

Entering Witney from behind its leisure centre, you are almost immediately in the Market Square at the heart of the town, with its beautiful Butter Cross dating from around 1600 beside the 18th-century Town Hall with its arcaded open ground floor. For centuries, Witney was famous for the production of woollen blankets. Although the blanket mills have now closed, the local football club, Witney FC, is still nicknamed 'The Blanketmen'.

You could stop for refreshments at The Fleece, with a view of the extensive town green, after which the walk takes you back past Witney Lake, a former gravel pit restored by Witney Town Council. This is now a nature reserve where you can see crested grebes and occasionally catch a glimpse of a kingfisher.

start / finish	The Square, Ducklington
nearest postcode	OX29 7UD
distance	4 miles / 6.4 km
time	2 hours
terrain	Mainly footpaths, which can get muddy after rain.

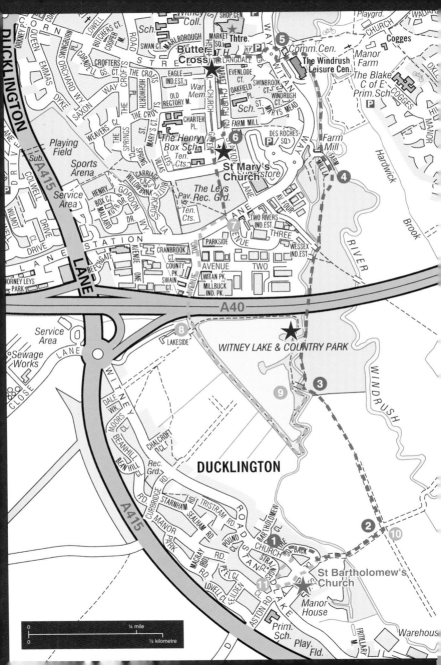

1 Park in or around The Square in Ducklington. Turn into Back Lane. Continue until the end of the lane and then turn left at the allotments beside the cemetery. Go through the gate along the footpath marked 'Witney 1', keeping the allotments on your right. Go over the bridge and straight on along a wide, cream-coloured path.

2 At the end of the path, turn left onto the Windrush Path (spot the interpretation board on the right-hand side at the turn). Walk alongside the field between the fence to the left and the hedge to the right and go through the gate at the end. Cross the field ahead of you following the path slightly to the left then go through another gate and along the path ahead.

3 At the fork, go to the right and continue on the Windrush Path and through another gate. You are now at Witney Lake and Country Park ★. Where the path forks again, go to the left and pass under the A40 along the underpass. After that, keep left across the field. Go through a metal gate on a path to the left of the field. Continue through the fields passing a bridge on your left.

4 Come to a gatepost on the left and an interpretation board entitled 'Witney Lake and Country Park'. Turn left and continue. Turn through the gate and go along a long path with the river to the right. Exit opposite a converted stone house, now flats, called The Old Mill and take the path on the right. The river is now in on your left and further on you will have water on both sides, both of which are branches of the River Windrush. Go across the wooden boardwalk and take the left fork, crossing a bridge on your left over the River Windrush. Pass an electricity station on your right.

5 Emerge at a roundabout on Witan Way. You'll have the leisure centre on your left. Cross the roundabout and go straight on to Langdale Gate road. Continue on the right-hand pavement between stone walls with the car park to the right. Turn left at the Butter Cross ★ and head along The Green towards St Mary the Virgin Church ★.

6 Turn right in front of the church and walk along the front of the church until you reach the entrance to the churchyard between the stone pillars. Head right and follow the path to the right of the church. Continue through the barriers and the white posts and across The Leys recreation ground.

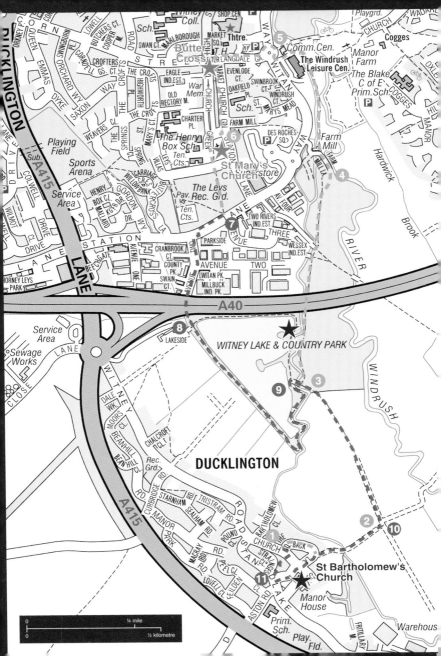

7 Turn right onto Station Lane and continue to the pedestrian crossing, past a children's playground on your right. Cross the pedestrian crossing and walk straight ahead into Station Lane Industrial Estate Avenue Two. Go straight on, passing Swain Court at the end of the road. Follow the path to the right along and under the underpass under the A40. Pass the bridge on the right and continue straight on to the lake.

8 Go through the gates into Witney Lake and Country Park. You will see the interpretation board on the right with the lake on the left. Continue straight on around the lake in an anticlockwise direction. Pass an electricity station on your right. Continue beyond the lake alongside a branch of the River Windrush, which leads you back towards the lake..

9 You will eventually come to a fork. Turn right and cross the bridge and follow the right-hand fork back. (You are now retracing your steps from the first part of the walk.) Go through the gate across the field directly ahead. Next, go right through the gate along the path, with the hedge on the left and the fence on the right.

10 At the bench, turn right and follow the path to the bridge. Cross the bridge and continue round to the gates beside the allotments. Instead of turning right back to The Square, continue straight ahead to find St Bartholomew's Church ★ , parts of which date from the 11th century. You can visit the church or continue straight ahead until you find Ducklington's delightful duck pond, usually amply populated with ducks.

11 Turn right past the Old School (now a private house) and right again into the yard of The Bell pub. This can be a last stop for refreshments, or you can walk directly through the yard and down a small alley to the left of the pub back to The Square.

⒜ walk twenty

A Taste of the Cotswolds

The picturesque villages of Minster Lovell and Crawley.

Just inside the Cotswolds Area of Outstanding Natural Beauty and 16 miles (26 km) from Oxford, the village of Minster Lovell is notable for its chocolate-box thatched cottages and magnificent ruins. The ruins of Minster Lovell Hall are picturesquely situated between a country church and a gently meandering river, and give off an air of ancient mystery. The first of the Lovell lineage (whose name was 'Lupellus' or 'little wolf') was granted land here by King Henry I in the 12th century. The ruins that are visible today are from the 15th century hall and you can walk around them identifying the rooms.

The walk starts at the Old Swan, a charming country pub which is now a hotel, up a street of thatched cottages, past the medieval church of St Kenelm and around its graveyard to the ruins.

From Minster Lovell Hall, you walk along the Windrush River and out into the countryside to the delightful village of Crawley. There are some pleasing views across the fields and woodland, particularly as you turn back from Crawley, and there are traditional country pubs in both villages should you require refreshment.

start / finish	Old Swan (pub), Minster Lovell
nearest postcode	OX29 0RN
distance	3½ miles / 5.6 km
time	1 hour 30 minutes
terrain	This walk can get very muddy, so wear suitable footwear if there has been any recent rain. Some steep slopes and stiles.

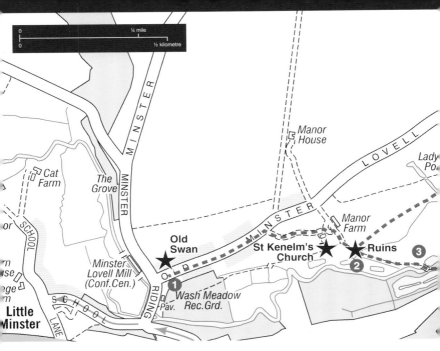

1 Park in the village. With your back to the Old Swan ★, turn left and walk along the road until you reach a small parking area. Turn right through the car park along a path. The path becomes a road. Turn right through St Kenelm's churchyard and go past the church ★ to its left. Continue through the graveyard and turn left towards the ruins of Minster Lovell Hall ★.

2 Walk through the ruins and exit at the left-hand corner of the site opposite where you came in. Go through the kissing gate by the board and take the right-hand fork. Then go through metal gates and across a small wooden bridge. Continue along the path through the field. Listen, and you will hear water beside you to the right.

3 Go through another metal gate and cross a longer wooden bridge over the River Windrush, then carry on left following the path. Continue along the riverbank. Turn right onto a boardwalk across a bit of river filled with rushes. Continue along the track on the left at slightly higher elevation through woodland and go through a metal gate.

4 Continue along the right-hand side of the field. Pass through another metal gate and carry on to the left-hand side of the field. Exit the field to the left via woodland, passing through a gap between a gate and the fence. Turn right up a steep slope in the wood. At the end of the woodland, go through metal gates across a field. Go straight on to another metal gate.

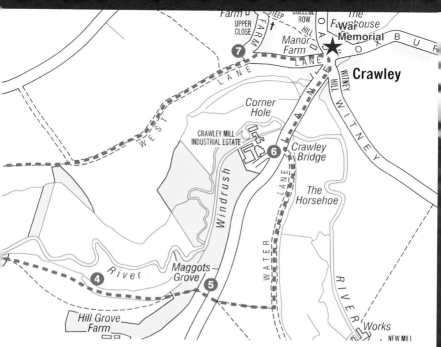

5 After the gate, cross the road and follow the path with a yellow footpath sign straight ahead. At the end of the field, turn left at the gate and stiles. Go into the woodland ahead. Continue along a very long path for about 15 minutes.

6 At the road, Dry Lane, cross a bridge into Crawley on the right. Continue along the road through Crawley. At the War Memorial, just before the Lamb Inn, turn left into Farm Lane and continue up the hill.

7 Turn left at Rose Cottage and follow the footpath sign. Walk alongside a sheep field with a view to the left of an industrial chimney. The path goes along a ridge and then descends. Continue straight on and cross a stile. At the fork, continue straight on.

8 Pass through fields until eventually you see the Minster Lovell Hall ruins ahead of you. Continue straight on, heading slightly to the left of the ruins. Go through the ruins and back through the graveyard to the lane leading to the High Street. Retrace your steps to the Old Swan.

images